Readers' experiences with the *Boo*[illegible]

"Wise, heart-centered...deeply nourishing. I [illegible] *while honoring individuality to be totally hap*[illegible] *at the current edge of our great unfolding."*

– **Elizabeth Lehman**, MA, MSW, LCSW, developer of Restoring Connection® With Life & Thriving (NYC and Warwick, NY)

"This series of books is wonderful and I will use them year after year, knowing that the more I use them, the deeper my understanding of the great mystery we call life will reveal itself to me and through me. I truly believe we can change the world by changing and understanding ourselves. This material provides the structure to do just that."

– **Stacie Florer**, jewelry artist, writer & teacher (Asheville, NC)

"My husband and I both work with the Wisdoms, and on many days the Angel offers just what we need to hear precisely when we need to hear it. We feel so completely companioned and in full awareness of the Angel presence."

– **Rev. Mary Gracely** (Houston, TX)

"Terah's Birth Angels books are fantastic, all of them! And my journey with the "dailies" has been profound...offering reminders, signposts, guidance for my daily living and interactions with my world. In this 5th volume, I'm inspired by the similarity with my own ministries and life orientation."

– **Aletheia M Mystea**, MA, psychotherapist & founder of Green Theology Ministries: Earth Rites, Animal Rites, Human Rites (Fort Collins CO)

"I look forward to starting my day by reading the Daily Wisdom as it opens my heart and instills loving awareness of what I need to focus on that day to allow my light to shine brightly out into the world."

– **Tina Wettengel**, physical therapist & spiritual teacher (Pittsburgh, PA)

"The Birth Angles Book of Days are treasures. They are prisms of wisdom, refracting enlightenment into each person's heart differently. What I love most about these books is that they focus me each day, illuminating a different part of consciousness to greet, to hone, to witness, and to love."

– **Lindy Labriola**, student, writer, singer-songwriter (Amherst, MA)

"This material has had a profound effect on me. The readings are so non-judgmental in tone that they've helped me to "zoom out" from day to day concerns and see the world painted in a much warmer, less threatening light."

– **Paula Mooney**, nurse, gardener & herbalist (Bigelow, AR)

BIRTH ANGELS

Book of Days

Daily Wisdoms with the 72 Angels of the Tree of Life

Volume 5: January 9 ~ March 20

Relationship with Community and the World

Terah Cox

Stone's Throw Publishing House
February 2015

BIRTH ANGELS BOOK OF DAYS

Daily Wisdoms with the 72 Angels of the Tree of Life
Volume 5: January 9 ~ March 20
Relationship with Community and the World

Series includes:
Volume 1: March 21 – June 2
Relationship with the Divine
Volume 2: June 3 – August 16
Relationship with Self
Volume 3: August 17 – October 29
Relationship with Work and Purpose
Volume 4: October 30 – January 8
Relationship with Others
Volume 5: January 9 – March 20
Relationship with Community and the World

Stone's Throw Publishing House
ISBN-13: 978-0692397817
ISBN-10: 0692397817
First Edition Softcover | Volume 5: February 2015
Kindle Digital Edition | Volume 5: February 2015

For permissions, information about author and additional books and materials, see
www.72BirthAngels.com
www.terahcox.com

Book design by Terah Cox
Wing detail of Fresco Angel by Giotto di Bondone,
Scenes from the Life of Christ #4 (1304-06)

Other Books by Terah Cox

BIRTH ANGELS BOOK OF DAYS ~ Vols. 1 - 4
Daily Wisdoms with the 72 Angels of the Tree of Life
Stone's Throw Publishing House (Vols. 1-4, 2014)
Vol. 1: March | Vol. 2: May | Vol. 3: August | Vol. 4: October

THE STORY OF LOVE & TRUTH
Stone's Throw Publishing House
Limited Handmade Edition (2007)
Illustrated Softcover Edition (2011)

BIRTH ANGELS ~ Fulfilling Your Life Purpose with the 72 Angels of the Kabbalah
Andrews McMeel/Simon & Schuster (2004)
(acquired by Stone's Throw Publishing House 2013)
Greek edition: Asimakis Publishing, Athens, Greece (2014)
Czech edition: Barevny Svet s.r.o (2016)

YOU CAN WRITE SONG LYRICS
Writers Digest / F&W Publications (2001)

For more information about the 72 Angels tradition, the Tree of Life, and Birth Angels with Terah Cox:
www.72BirthAngels.com

For permissions, additional works and information about author:
www.terahcox.com

Table of Contents

Gratitudes

As Volume 5 now completes this series, I am so grateful to my "inner co-creators" for their loving steadiness of presence – especially for being here even when I'm not! In their uncanny ways of guiding me back into the eternal present, they have also continually led me to people, moments and other sources that have helped to support and clarify their inner tuitions when I needed perspective from the outer world. As the 72 "Angles" of Divine Light illuminate again and again, remarkable capacities of feeling, knowing, being and doing are available to all of us when we do what we humanly do in co-creation with our inner Divine.

Throughout the writing of this series I had been wishing for a connection in Spain that could provide more background information on Haziel and Kabaleb, whose 20th century works I have used as sources for certain aspects of the 72 Angels tradition. Just as I was completing this last volume, I received an email out of the "Angelic blue" from Linda Wheeler Bryant in Madrid, who happened to mention that her teacher was the daughter of Kabaleb! As it turns out, three of Kabaleb's children are carrying on his legacy since his death in 1991. Linda connected me first to Milena Llop, and then Kabaleb's son Tristan, who both provided a wealth of information on their father, with input from Soleika Llop. Enrique Llop (writing and teaching as Kabaleb), was a journalist, Kabbalah scholar, esoteric astrologer, author and founder of E.T.U, La Escuela de Transcendentalista Universal. Kabaleb's works, some of which were published in France under the name of his student and long-time friend Haziel, helped to reawaken the 72 Angels tradition in Spain and France in the 20th century. Kabaleb's children continue his work through their own professions and in publishing additional works of their father – Tristan Llop: author, Kabbalah astrologer and teacher in the 72 Angels tradition, as well as director of ETU (www.nuevavibracion.com); Milena Llop: journalist, transpersonal psychologist, Kabbalah teacher and astrologer in the 72 Angels tradition (www.redmilenaria.com); and Soleika Llop: author of *Alquimia Genetica*, *Los Dioses Internos,* and *Los Angeles al Alcance de Todos,* co-authored with Kabaleb, as well as a practitioner of Kabbalah astrology and developer of a unique therapy in genetic alchemy (www.alchemiagenetica.com.es).

These connections to Kabaleb have helped me to understand how certain aspects of the 72 Angels tradition developed from the medieval and Renaissance Kabbalah to the present day. Thus, thank you Milena and Soleika for your input, and Tristan especially for the lively and illuminating hours of Skype conversation. Finally, Linda, none of this would have been possible without your openness to hear and answer my request to the universe with your kind generosity in bringing us together!

I am also very thankful that I found the online posting of a speech given by Dartmouth Professors and celebrated travel writers, Myrna Katz Frommer and Harvey Frommer, in which they discuss the excavations in Gerona, Spain of a long-hidden medieval Kabbalah school and community that had been walled up by the Spanish Inquisition in 1492. Their information connects yet another dot in the history and evolution of the Kabbalah (see Appendix II). (Santangel 98 International Symposium: The Spanish-Jewish Connection: A Resurgence of a Community that Never Died, Dominican University, River Forest, Illinois, August 1998, posted at www.dartmouth.edu/~frommer/s_j_connection.htm).

To those who contributed your comments and stories to this volume, thank you Stacie Florer, Paula Mooney, Lindy and Sara Labriola, Mary Gracely, Elizabeth Lehmann, Tina Wettengel, Aletheia Mystea and Annie Britt Shaw – and for all those far and wide who have supported the *Book of Days* project from the beginning with your reviews, patronage, encouragement and word-of-heart-and-mouth. Many thanks also to those patients ones who signed up to receive the Daily Wisdoms via email while I've been completing this volume 5:

Aletheia Mystea, Annie Shaw, Arnie Roman & Tanya Leah, Beth Askew, Beth Smith, Cathleen O'Connor, Chuck Pisa, Cindy Cox, Claudia Duchene, Dan Koppel, Eleonora Kouvoutsaki, Elizabeth Lehman, Ephrem Holdener, Fan Michail Anurag, Gilberto Costa, Go Ming Oi, Imogene Drummond, Isobel Stamford, Janice Tuchinsky, Jodi Tomasso, Jose Ramos, Judith Clements, Kelly Klamut, Laura Gould, Laura Parisi, Lindy Labriola, Mary Gracely, Michael Anastas, Paula Mooney, Rebecca Mitchell, Reina Pinel, Sarah Gallant, Sharon Etienne, Stacie & Shayne Florer, Stephanie Lodge, Sue Heiferman, Teri Barr, Tina Wettengel, Yuta Kubareva...and many more.

Finally, my gratitude abounds for family and friends who continue to be so supportive and co-creative, in your different ways, to my life and work: Stacie Florer, Jodi Tomasso, Arnie Roman, Tanya Leah, Chuck Pisa, Teri Barr, Amy Zachary, Paula Mooney, the Delzells, Honey Kirila, Davina Long, Paxton McAbee, Cathleen O'Connor, Saskia Shakin, Dave Robbins, Dominic Petrillo, Teresa Peppard, Gittel Price, Donna Zucchi, Elizabeth Hepburn, Ken Appleman, Bob Tomasso, goddaughters Lindy and Sara and their parents Art and Stacy Labriol; my nieces Bekah Hicks and Hannah Zeno, Aramis and Aden Zeno, and my sisters Cindy Cox and Connie Hicks.

Preface

The almost two years I have been working on this 5-volume *Book of Days* has been a long inner winter of co-creation with the 72 "Angles" of the Divine Light to bring forth the Daily Wisdoms. Just as with a baby in the gestation cradle of the womb, we don't really know what we have until it is fully birthed. Now that the fifth volume is coming to a close and the core messages of the Daily Wisdoms are coalescing within me, I'm realizing that in 365 different ways, we are being invited to live and co-create in the light of awareness that **we are never "only human," but Divine-Human beings**. In every moment of life we are being given the opportunity – especially during times of pain and challenge – to awaken to the Divine that dwells within our humanity and use it to support and "super-charge" our lives. If we cultivate a continual space of awareness within us for that knowing, then we will come to understand the fullness of who we truly are, why we're here, and what gifts we hold for the world.

What I have experienced on this co-creative journey is that because the challenges, responsibilities, pleasures and pains of human life are so compelling, we must renew the awareness of our inner Divine again and again, every day, from moment to moment. And this is what the Daily Wisdoms are for – tools for opening our hearts and minds to re-mind us of what we already know in our innermost beings – that we are more than all this, and it is that "more" of us that gives all the rest of it meaning.

Most of us do not arrive at a perfected state of enlightenment here on this Earth. I think it's likely that we're not here to do so – but rather to play and re-play the excruciating and joyful challenge of tapping into and applying our Divine soul-nature to every human relating, challenge and potential we encounter. I have found that while the epiphany-moments of realization, creation and mystical experience can give the seminal thrust we need to crack our hearts and minds open to let in more light, **it is the practice of**

repetition – bringing the light into more and more scenarios – that increases and deepens our awareness. Of course, along the way, a few spectacular "light-bulb moments" here and there can keep us enthusiastically going!

Until this project, I have never committed to a daily practice of anything. While truth-seeking through listening, speaking and writing has been my lifelong work, I've always done the writing part in fits and starts, with bursts of intense productivity around starting and finishing a project. Writing these Daily Wisdoms every day has *forced* me to deal consistently with all the colors of my own "hue-manity" – especially the challenge of "re-coloring" the gray days with the rest of the rainbow when all I could feel and see were shades of gray, so to speak. Thus, I have revisited each of the Daily Wisdoms again and again to re-color any leakage of gray within them by bringing myself in a different light – the light that loving brings when we bring love to whatever we do. For only in a state of love am I able to feel and hear the Angelic and their messages.

I am looking forward over the next year to the practice of using these Wisdoms myself as a reader and partaker. I anticipate that as the Angelic presences deepen and my own awareness increases, there will be changes in the messages. Just as we ourselves are not written in stone, neither is anything we create. When we bring love to our creations, they become living and energetic transmitters of love. And I imagine that as you continue to engage with them and your awareness increases, there will be changes in you too, so that you will understand them differently in each new season of your life.

As my friend and colleague Stacie Florer worked with the Daily Wisdoms from one volume to the next over this last year, she commented that the progression of the themes for each volume seemed to be "perfect." From our relationship to the Divine, and then with the self, our work and purpose, our close family and friend circles, and then the world at large – the self is revealed as cause and impetus for what the world ultimately becomes. Stephen Cope, in his book, *The Greatest Work of Your Life,* seems to concur:

> Our actions in expression of our dharma – my actions, your actions, everyone's actions – are infinitely important. They connect us to the soul of the world. They create the world. Small as they may appear, they have the power to uphold the essential inner order of the world. (p. 47)

I was a little worried with the writing of this Volume 5 that it would be a big departure from the personal issues of the first four volumes. Here, we are asked to bring our awareness and who we are to a world stage that many of us would often rather ignore for all the precarious conditions that feel so much bigger than our ability to impact. However, the Angel Wisdoms tell us that our power to change the world is in the "awakening numbers" of individuals.

Every condition in our world was initiated by individuals, and thus cures for the world's ills must also start with us as individuals. This has been especially demonstrated in the tragic events that have occurred during the creation of this volume, which include not only the escalating brutality of the so-called Islamic State – but the *Charlie Hebdo*, Copenhagen and other violent attacks orchestrated by what the media calls self-radicalized "lone-wolf" individuals.

It has been hard – and yet uncannily timely – to watch these atrocities happening while working on this volume. And yet with each happening I felt and heard the Angel in my heart illuminating the deeper lessons about how the darker and hurting aspects of our global psyche are showing us where healing is needed within all of us. For as the dark comes to the surface and into the light, it can be seen for what it is and addressed. With sober joy, I have watched the global conversation progress from outrage and blame to **a question of collective responsibility for what happens in our world**. This is the overlighting message of Volume 5.

From the perspective of the Angel Wisdoms, we have tremendous power as individuals to save our world – and thus we must attend to each other's hurts. We must bring our personal values – our inner sense of what is good and true and right for ourselves and our loved ones – into the greater world of our neighbors near and far, our workplaces, organizations, governments and diverse cultures. We can start with the quality of relatings we are willing to have with each other, and in our courage to explore each other's unknowns and find not only the other, but also ourselves. For the soul of the world is hurting, and only we, in our aware and willing togetherness, can heal it.

* * *

We may have come on different ships,

but we're in the same boat now.

~ Martin Luther King, Jr.

* * *

Introduction

The Daily Wisdoms in this last volume of the *Book of Days* speak to us about how we bring ourselves, our individuation and personal realms to the world-at-large and the collective consciousness. Each of our unique ways of being, doing, relating, perceiving and purposing have tremendous impact on how we affect and *effect* each other at every level of life, including our relationship with the Earth that sustains us. As seeds in the soil of humanity, what we make of ourselves we are making of the world. How we see and feel about ourselves is what we see and feel about the world – which, as quantum physics says, impacts how and what the world becomes, for better or worse.

Awareness is key, the Wisdoms tell us again and again – awareness first of all, and foundationally, that we are not "only human," but Divine-Human beings. Our entire lives, the eternal soul-spark that is our inner Divine is trying to be heard, seen and felt in order to have co-creative time and place in our outer human expressions and creations. In coming to realize and embrace this spiritual fact of our humanity, we come to see ourselves, each other and all of life in a different light.

This important central message that runs through the Daily Wisdoms was reiterated for me in a webcast interview with Andrew Harvey that I happened to catch in the last couple of days of completing this volume. Andrew's remarkable work over many years has coalesced into the illumination of Jesus' teachings without the trappings of religion, which he calls "The Christ Path." Within the first few minutes of this particular webcast he said, "this time is about the birth of the divine human...uniting the inner with the outer...our inner divine with the derelictions of our humanity." He went on to say that ultimately our "baptism in Divine consciousness" becomes "love in action on every level..."

In its most active role, love is indeed an action verb! As the Wisdoms say, "*truth may know what's wrong with the world, but only love can change it.*" The "sacred activism" that Harvey proffers is the action of a love that is utterly committed to the rehabilitation of our humanity through reconciliation with our inner Divine. For only in the commingling of the Divine and the human will we remember that truly, we are all interconnected on the inside. And like "*leaves on the same family tree of life,*" as the Wisdoms say, we come to realize that "*whatever help or hurt is done to one is done to all.*"

This oneness-memory is held within our souls and broadcast to our hearts continually. Yet, this high-vibrational love-and-light-message of oneness is easily drowned out by the heavier, darker cacophony and relentless insistence of a competitive outer world. The key is to commit ourselves to practices that return us to soul awareness daily and from moment to moment in the relatings, encounters and circumstances of our lives.

As awareness of our relatedness to all beings and events grows, we begin to recognize the shadows within us in play on the global stage, in multiplied proportions. We see what our personal desire to own more and more stuff does to rainforests, farmlands and oceans. Or how our secret little racial or gender biases escalate into hate crimes and the deaths of unarmed teenagers. We see the compromise of our integrity and personal values in the corruption of our corporations and governments. And how marginalization of certain peoples robs all of us of well-being and the richness that diversity brings to the entirety of humanity. And how our suspicions and intolerances of people who have different beliefs ultimately cultivate the world's ideological killing fields.

Most of us tend to be wrapped up in the dramas and dreams of our own lives. But the world, and our precious privilege of Earth, need us to begin to shift our consciousness to an understanding of how important to the whole is the right use of our individual powers and purposes. Whatever difficult things happen in our world, in one way or another we all contribute to the cause – and thus we must all contribute to the cure. For it is not about blame, the Wisdoms tell us. Rather it's about love, compassion and "response-ability" for our kind, and for conditions in the world that have been compounded by the generations which every new generation must do its part to heal.

The Angel Wisdoms especially draw our attention to how our thoughts, feelings and actions impact the natural world. As our host and vital ally, the Earth is continually exampling to us how to live more harmoniously with each other – and how to be resilient in weathering the storms of life, the winds of change and the seasons and cycles of life's comings and goings. This is important not only for our own greater expression and fulfillment, but also in bringing "better and better" versions of ourselves to the world.

The latter half of winter (for those of us who dwell in the northern hemisphere) is the season of the year when the natural world encourages us to go within to ruminate, re-evaluate, formulate and gestate whatever is next for us. This invisible part of our rebirthing is vital for the shaping of our ongoing renewal. In the dark womb of our own within, we have access to the spiritual energies and purposes which are carried in our souls and broadcast to our hearts. As our knowledge and experience are commingled with love and compassion, the light-seeds of new becomings begin to amass substance and momentum. Soon, as the flora and fauna of the natural world are quickened by the warming light of the sun – the light of our own awareness quickens our gestative process. Finally, and seemingly overnight, we emerge with newborn beingness, new energies, attitudes and outlooks, new endeavors and a new sense of who, how, what and why we want to be in the world.

As so many thought leaders, visionaries, teachers, healers and world issues are broadcasting to us in these times, it is vital that we come to realize how important we are as individuals to collective humanity and everything that happens in our world. For better or worse, the seeds we cultivate in our own inner and outer gardens are disseminated by both the seen and unseen currents of interconnection throughout all of humanity and the natural world. Will the hues we bring forth in our own blossoming contribute to the flowering hues of possibility in the world? Or will we muddy the colors of everyone's potential through limiting and fearful thoughts, actions and un-creations?

At every moment, we are given opportunities to save the world by loving it. If not us, then who, will do it? And if not now, when?

Seeds in the Soil of Humanity

According to the ageless wisdoms, our souls come to Earth again and again to fulfill certain purposes and potentials. Many of these – such as learning, healing and balancing the effects of our actions – are said to be common to all souls. However, part of the delight of human life is the different ways and contexts in which each of us do those same things as per the variable qualities and dynamics of our individual human will, beingness and life circumstances.

Our multiple lifetimes give us opportunities to literally "walk in another man's shoes" – even if that means in some cases that we go shoeless. It is said that if we do harm to someone in one life, our souls may choose to come into another life as someone who experiences a similar harm so that we can better understand the effects of our actions upon others. Rarely, it is said, do we come here to just rest and have everything go our way. Because the vibrational density of physical life can dull us to our soul reality, our deeper learning and awareness are often most accelerated through contrast and adversity. In these we choose situations that almost "force" us to remember our inner Divine resources, so that we might not only withstand our very human challenges and trials – but also triumph.

In each life, we learn to apply what we learned in previous lifetimes, roles and scenarios – much the same way in which our same life-lessons keep coming up in different scenarios just in the span of this one lifetime. With all of this, we would hopefully create better and better versions of the world, too.

One Seed, a Whole Field

Who we are and what more we become is vital to the greater potential of humanity and the conditions of our world. Events and messages of significance throughout humankind's history have always been initiated by individuals first – and then often taken up by groups and organizations who tacked on their own agendas and motives – even to the point of distorting the truth and integrity of the original message. No religion or tradition on the planet has been immune to this, nor has any government or nation, nor likely most organizations or corporations.

Ultimately, the prevailing consciousness of individual leaders is magnified in the phenomenon of group energy until it becomes bigger than any one individual. Once that happens, the group has its own collective mind, which breeds thought-forms that, according to their vibrational qualities, can positively affect, or negatively infect, individual and group thoughts, motives and behavior. Like a snowball rolling down a hill, as they keep going and gaining momentum the group energies continue to accumulate, influencing a wider and wider net of people.

In groups and organizations, you can usually discern the quality of leadership by the enthusiasm and commitment – or lack thereof – of its members or employees. The positive energies of healthy, honorable, focused, well-motivated and generous leadership "trickles-down" to everyone in the group – enabling those individuals in supporting roles to feel a sense of value and personal integrity in contributing to something worthwhile. Thus, because of the compounded positive energy of the group, goals will likely not only be met but exceeded, with results that return even more positive energy and rewards to the group. And if such a group hits "hard times," there is a willingness to bear the burden of difficulties together – from the top down.

On the other "side," when leadership is using a group merely to satisfy its own self-interested agendas of greed and power, supporting personnel will be unhappy, argumentative and poorly productive. Over time they may become depressed, and even physically ill, from having to work within the constant bombardment of life-negating energies and a distorted value system that is offensive to them personally.

Our David-and-Goliath world. Corporations and governments often seem 'larger than life' and beyond the reach of change by individuals. As they become giant machines that seem to run *us*, there is a tendency for mission statements, ethics and bottom lines to degrade into serving the interests of the few, while the individuals who support and should be benefiting from them become more and more subservient and depleted. But trying to change a group is like trying to turn an ocean liner at a 90-degree angle on a dime – and in the meantime a little boat can run circles around it. While corporations and governments are technically made up of individuals, even those at the helm can become handicapped by the overriding necessity of meeting bottom lines and profit margins. Mix that with a constant rub, say, between even honorable goals, but impure motives and means – compounded by internal dissension – and group effectiveness slows way down.

And so what is the solution? How do we stop these runaway trains that we (humankind) create in which we feel less and less like passengers and more like sacrificial lambs tied to the tracks?

The power of one times the many. The Angel Wisdoms suggest that although we may often feel little and powerless against the behemoths of our own creations – our power as individuals is in **our awakening numbers**. In the rise and expansion of our individual and ultimately collective awareness, we come to realize that we can only be manipulated if we are continually apathetic, dulled or distracted. One of the great attention-gobblers in our consumer societies is having our need for immediate gratification constantly fed. As long as we have what we need and want in our daily lives, we tend to not pay attention to what's going on in the rest of the world. Thus, it is often only when global affairs affect our daily personal lives that we begin to take notice.

According to Wikipedia.org there have been 47 recessions just in America since 1790. Most recently, during the worst years of the 2007-2009 recession when people in America were losing jobs and homes at rapid-fire rates, suddenly we looked up to ask what was going on "at the top" that was causing such significant disturbance in our personal lives. Soon, of course, what was happening to us ultimately created a ripple effect on the economies of Europe and beyond. The opportunity in all this? We woke up – at least a little bit.

We became more aware of greed, corruption, the misuse of power and the manipulations by the self-interested few to exploit the many – and we demanded change. Ultimately we got at least some change because consumer buying power was weakened, and thus big business felt the bite. Those of us who lost a lot learned to recognize the blessings of what we still had. Many of us used our limited means to boost our creativity, start over and build things that had more meaning for us. We began to cultivate a hunger for something deeper, realizing that our needs could not always be assured in the shallows of "stuff and more stuff." We also came to realize that in coming together with other individuals who are awake and aware, our effect in the world multiplies and accumulates. Together, we can have more say, and if we keep at it we may ultimately get back more and more control over having our personal life-affirming values implemented in corporate and government protocols, bottom lines and accountability.

I don't think solutions are about eradicating corporations and governments, but rehabilitating and renewing them with individual initiatives, missions and principles that are life-affirming and regenerating for all. As I was writing this, I saw a Tokyo news segment about the CEO of Japanese Airlines who lowered his own very moderate salary to mitigate layoffs and other economic and work-load stress on company employees during difficult times. He said that his business experience has shown that "a company that always puts money first will eventually fail." In the meantime, big business in the west is full of CEOs who collect multi-million dollar salaries while their companies slowly tank and the cost of goods becomes more and more inflated.

The Power of Awareness

Sometimes we feel there is so much that needs to be done that anything we might do will be just a drop in the desert. But it is our awareness, and our willingness to do *something,* that initiate energies of intention and thought-forms that accumulate exponentially – ultimately having reach and effect far beyond us.

The Wisdom of the Angel MEBAHIAH (Intellectual Lucidity) suggests:

> *...become more and more aware of what is happening around you and in your world. For it is the power of awareness, along with your desire to see something more loving and whole, that starts the energetic ripple of possibility for shift to happen. Many of you hold shame about seeing without committing to action for change. But no, no! – even just your seeing is powerful – especially when you see with love and mercy, rather than judgment of yourself or others. ...Hold space within your own heart for the healing of the world, and take that healing awareness into your day through the way you do what you do and the kindness you show to family, friends and colleagues. Changing the world can be that simple, and that profound.*

Thanks to our rapidly advancing technologies, citizen news reporters, videographers and social networking, awareness of global issues is something we would have to work to avoid! What I am discerning from different streams of information is that the solutions are already happening because of the growing awareness of what needs to change. As more and more organizational corruption is exposed, there are more visionary voices and calls to action rising out of the fray. Some of these individuals are coming together to form small but increasingly powerful groups which operate from a point of higher consciousness for a greater and more sustainable good. Through volunteers and "crowd-funding" donations – asking a lot of people for a little bit of support – their "awareness-in-action" initiatives offer visionary solutions that aim at the thriving of each and all – including the Earth.

What is the ideal goal? To summarize the different ways the 72 Angels say it in this volume, it would be this: Stop taking from the many to give to only a few – but rather partake of the attributes, talents and knowledge of each so that the parts and the whole of humanity may become interdependent, and thus more vibrant and self-sustaining to each and all for the long-term. For ultimately, "*none can truly thrive unless all thrive.*"

Our Personal Global World

So what does group awareness, collective consciousness and cooperation mean for you and me as individuals and neighbors near and far? We are not all inclined to stand at podiums as thought leaders, visionaries or activists or join movements for global change. For most of us, our world-at-large has long been our circle of friends and business colleagues, community activities and *maybe* world news. However, for many of us across the world our increasing use of social media is widening our circles and giving us a sense of belonging with the rest of the world, and a feeling of home, wherever we happen to be. My friend Stacie Florer – who uses social networking daily to share her jewelry art and her sensibilities about life, meaning and connection on both personal and business levels – has observed how social media is helping to change what we feel and think about different cultures through personal one-on-one connections.

> My worldview has changed a lot with the popularity of social media platforms. I can take a photo of a meaningful, albeit small moment in my day, and have an online friend living in another country share it with her friends, and within minutes my moment has crossed multi-national borders and time zones. I think that in the borderless reality of the online world we are transitioning from thinking about our home as it relates to a fixed border into a home that includes the rest of the world. With a growing awareness that, at lightning speed, our lives DO affect others around the world, it seems that social media could be a precursor to an actual borderless world.

In talking about this with Stacie, it's as if our virtual online world is somewhat akin to the world of thought before it becomes manifested into reality. Imagine a truly borderless world! "Imagine...the world...as one...a brotherhood of man," John Lennon's song suggested to our collective hearts and minds some 44 years ago. This song, with its emotional appeal to our inner oneness-memory, seeded our 20th century consciousness in ways that helped to open us to the rest of the world – especially to Eastern traditions which promote a spiritual state of being and a sense of unity. Now, a couple of generations later, what was an exotic foray into global spiritual love has seeped into the growing consciousness of a youth that is curious about each other's cultures and ways.

My goddaughter Sara's global world began with her discovery online of "world music," which led her to studying the sitar with an Indian master at a New York ashram, then the thrill of meeting Ravi Shankar's daughter – and now a dream to go to India. Last summer her global world was playing gypsy jazz guitar at a Paris music festival with musicians from all over the world. From a small village in upstate New York, Sara's outreach into the world via her world-music interests and her multi-cultural connections have helped to expand her consciousness in a way that makes her interested in – not afraid or suspicious of – people who are different from her, but also, as she says, "the same."

Today my global world is exchanging emails with someone in Europe about the 72 Angels, sending the Daily Wisdoms out to readers across the world via email, and an Israeli singer-songwriter friend and sometime collaborator, David Broza, whose DVD documentary, "East Jerusalem, West Jerusalem" just arrived in the mail this afternoon. David's global world has been a lifelong mission to reconcile Jews and Muslims through his multicultural recordings and worldwide performances, often in areas of conflict.

My older goddaughter Lindy and her high-school classmates did a summer trip to a small Peruvian village a few years ago to help build a school, teach English, repair field irrigation systems and construct water purification filters. I asked her when she returned what was most notable for her about the trip. She said it was how happy the people were – and it wasn't attached to having things, because they didn't have anything really except each other and what they needed for basic survival. And, she said, it was also how they all helped each other, from the smallest to the eldest, and not just within their own families, but in their little community. It was all just so simple, she said – not about having or doing worldly things, but just being with each other and the day, whatever it brought.

Lindy is at a college now which requires high academic achievement and draws applications from students all around the world. I asked her about how her multi-cultural sensibilities have developed since she's been there.

> Most of the international students are extremely motivated to succeed academically. It was so difficult for many of them to get here from the countries they lived in. Their discipline has motivated me a lot because it made me realize how often people take education for granted when it is not only uncommon, but sometimes impossible for many families in third world countries to send their kids to college. I have a friend from an extremely poor family in Vietnam who taught herself high level math so that she could get a full scholarship here. Now she does research for some of the best math and science professors at the college.

Educational opportunity is an incredible means for world change. As the saying goes, people fear what they don't understand. Exposing ourselves and our children to other cultures and ways ultimately leads us to discover the sameness behind our differences, which is the clue and the *glue* to the greater reality of our underlying unity. While concepts like "separation of church and state" have helped to maintain religious freedoms, they have also prevented us from learning about each other's ways and beliefs, thus contributing to bias and divisiveness.

Again, most of us aren't world leaders who can wave a political wand or conduct some kind of back room negotiation that will change the world for the better in one fell swoop. Not that that could likely happen anyway, because for every public person and podium there seems to be a gaggle of conflicting private interests and hidden agendas that at the very least greatly affect what goes on in the world.

Rather, the kind of systemic change that our world needs, and which is immediately possible for all of us to contribute toward, is done one person at a time meeting another person at the heart with willingness, compassion, integrity, respect, curiosity, kindness and participation in cooperative efforts with our particular skills and talents. And this can have an even greater impact when it's also a meeting of different cultures – recognizing and appreciating both our diversity and our mutual humanity.

There are many unsung remarkable individuals, thinkers and communicators among our ranks. Everyone has a message from their own life experiences that can benefit our world in some way. Again, I think the social media phenomenon has been a tremendous, culture-changing vehicle for this. I am amazed and encouraged at the abundance of positive, life-affirming portrayals of people inspiring and helping each other – along with the exposure of corruption and bad behavior which increases awareness and a rising insistence for justice, change and healing. There is also increasing awareness and concern for the well-being of the Earth and all her creatures. I find the videos of people helping animals, and animals of different species befriending and helping each other to be powerful examples of how we should be living and co-creating together – including with the Earth itself.

I recently read on Facebook that the nation of Bolivia is in the process of passing a "Law of the Rights of Mother Earth," giving it the status of a "legal personality" with the same rights as a human citizen to life and well-being. Researching further, I discovered that Bolivia follows in the footsteps of Ecuador, which in 2007-2008 passed unprecedented legislation adopting "Rights of Nature" to their constitution. This legislation recognizes that the natural world is not "property under the law," but that "nature in all its life forms has the right to exist, persist, maintain and regenerate its vital cycles." (www.therightsofnature.org) This movement is being generated especially by agronomic cultures whose livelihood and well-being rely heavily on the longevity of the Earth's health and well-being – rather than how much they can exploit and chemically force it to produce in as short a time as inhumanly possible!

In western countries inclined to urban living and technological emphasis, we have taken for granted our food supplies. And in the absence of our attention, some terribly exploitative companies have gained dangerous ground. With little to no legislative sanctions, these companies pollute our farmlands with poisonous chemicals and acquire patents on nature's seeds so that they can genetically modify them, to the detriment of food quality and the health of humans and animals. The good news is that more and more of us are paying attention now. And more of us are growing our own gardens and supporting local farmers' who grow organically. A great example of the power of individuals multiplied!

All solutions start with awareness. And all it takes is one person with awareness to start the flow of change. As the Angel Wisdom for ASALIAH says,

> *...your individual ideals and envisionings help to seed the kind of world you would like it to become. The challenge is to not invest, identify with or engage in negative events – or even fight them – but to hold a template within your heart and mind for what you want to see materialize so that your awareness and attention become a magnet for intention and fulfillment.*

Awareness commingled with intention is like our finger on the first domino, a stone thrown into a pond, a smile at a stranger, a pay-it-forward act of kindness. We don't always see the energetic ripples that we set into motion or where they wind up. But they are there, and they are still rippling, even unto the coming generations and the cosmos.

Different Ships...Same Boat

The words of Martin Luther King, Jr. quoted in the front of this volume – "We may have come on different ships, but we're in the same boat now" – apply to every collective, organization and nation that is composed of diverse people from diverse places and walks of life who have come together to accomplish a similar goal or mission. Even when we disagree about how to do that mission – and we always do – if we want to bring the boat to shore then we're going to have to work together – or all of us will drown. Working together doesn't mean doing the same things in the same way, but encouraging and drawing from each other's unique talents, skills and knowledge to do every different task needed to get the job done.

Separateness and Unity

This is one of the great paradoxes of our lives on Earth: the need for seeming separateness in order to express our individual choices, purposes, potentials and ways of being – and the simultaneous need to experience belonging and a sense of togetherness. To make it even more difficult, we often have mixed and even guilty feelings about whichever of these we are *not* doing at any given time – sometimes feeling selfish or unloving to others if we are focusing on our own individuation, and empty and dissatisfied if we're not.

Through an underlying sense of unity, however, we can support and benefit each other with our individuations, which will ultimately benefit all. Thus, the "answer" to this paradox is that we are here to do both and all of it – neither in complete dependence nor independence, but *interdependence.* And our greatest ongoing example of this is right under our feet and all around us.

Unknowingly to so many of us who live in urban areas, the natural world is always offering us understandings of life's mysteries – especially about how to cohabit with each other. So let's take a lesson about interdependence from the trees in the natural settings of our forests.

Trees each have their particular space – standing not so close that they stifle each other, but not so far that they can't shelter each other in a storm. And though they seem to stand separately, their root systems below ground are vastly interconnected, with an elder "mother tree" as the hub. With new saplings, or when one is stressed by systemic or environmental conditions, the others send it nutrients and life-giving energies. And when it's stronger, it contributes its energies and nutrients to others in the group as needed. (www.cryptik.squarespace.com/home/the-consciousness-of-trees.html)

As I've previously mentioned, I experienced uncanny nature communications and "inner tuitions" for a number of years whenever I would go forest-walking in the Hudson Highlands of upstate New York. On one of those walks the paradoxical subject of separateness and unity was addressed with the example of fire and water.

> *Together, fire and water extinguish each other. It is only in their separateness that each may come into the full glory of their potential. ... You come here to fulfill a unique purpose in ways that are different from others – and for that you need your own physical time and place. And therefor, be just separate enough on the outside, knowing that you can return to unity at any time by meeting each other inside, at the heart, where your sameness lies.*

This same message has been reiterated these many years later through some of the Angel wisdoms. ANAUEL (Perception of Unity) says:

> *You may live as seemingly separate leaves on humanity's family tree of life, each catching the light in your own ways – but it is the tree itself which sustains you. Thus, when you tap the resources of unity, you can draw from the eternal well of omniscience held within your soul and the souls of all others to aid you with matters in time and 'super-charge' your awareness, knowledge and experience.*

In our need to return to "the memory of unity which is held within [our] heart and soul," ANAUEL goes on to say,

> *There is often a push and pull in human thought between the concepts of unity and separation, as if they are mutually exclusive or that separation is an illusion or a 'bad' thing. We would like to shed some light on that.* ***The human life of your Divine soul is about the paradox of living in both contexts at once – in which the 'format' of separateness exists within the greater reality, or wholeness, of unity.*** *...Thus, here is the resolution to the paradox:* ***When you learn to embrace both unity and individuation as two sides of the Divine-Human 'coin' that you are, so to speak, you will discover the joy of your differences without feeling separate.***

The Sacred Role of Diversity

The cosmic mystery at the heart of this paradox of separateness and unity is that each of us come here not only for the evolution of our own souls, but simultaneously to express and expand an aspect, or constellation of qualities, of the Divine Itself. As the Daily Wisdoms illuminate, the diversity of humankind is a reflection of the Divine Oneness which "in the beginning" diversified into the many of creation. In so doing, the Kabbalah says, the inherent diverse nature of the Divine was revealed to Itself and expressed within, through and as each different created thing and being. Through diversity comes the contrast that sparks relationship and unlimited configurations of potential and growth for both the Divine and the human. Through our own uniqueness we may know which aspects of the Divine we are here to particularly express and expand (which is what our personal Birth Angels help to reveal to us). And just as we may often know ourselves better through the reflective eyes of the other upon us and through our own creations, so it was and continues to be for the Divine Itself.

Thus, each different soul, as a Divine-Human being in the "separateness nature" of physical life, is given time and place to explore its powers and potentials and the fulfillment of Divine-Human co-creativity on Earth. As the ANAUEL Wisdom details:

> *By virtue of every soul which is a 'light-spark' of the Divine Oneness, here you each are in a unique physical vehicle with the paradoxical Divine-Human purpose to* ***indivi****duate particular aspects of what is essentially* ***indivi****sible (the Divine Oneness). Thereby the Divine and all that IS may continually evolve and expand as you fulfill the particular glory of your unique potential.*

Through our individuation, we each bring particular aspects of the Heavens to Earth and create endless variables with them. That is what we are here to do. The problems come, however, when we inflate our unique experiences, preferences and beliefs to "gospel" status – especially our understandings of That Which we call by so many different names. Intolerance for our ideological and religious differences, and the need to define any one truth as an "only truth" and compel others accordingly, are at the root of so much of the violence and harm that has occurred throughout the history of humankind. And of course, it's still occurring.

The diversity of "Truth." Much has been said in the Angel Wisdoms about the "absolute" and "relative" natures of Truth, and the need of many to believe that their particular experience of truth is an "only" and "immutable" truth. This is somewhat natural to both fervor and fear, and the need for certainty in our constantly changing world. Through the centuries, however, **this need to affix an "only truth" to our relationship with the Divine has prevented many from entering into the deeper realms of the Divine mysteries and our own greater Divine-Human powers and potentials**. In many ways, especially early on, it has been more expedient to leave God up to the experts(!), and to follow (or not) dogmas and belief systems that other humans have formulated and prescribed.

However, there have always been individual questioners and seekers called to different paths and understandings, and every age has had its truth-beacons who have been the great lights in the history of our world. Mainstream religions have lost some of their hold on our collective psyches, especially in western countries, for a variety of reasons. I would venture to say that from the late 1800's to the present day, our world has seen an unprecedented exodus of traditional believers from churches, temples, mosques and more to pursue more personal and non-denominational paths of spiritual individuation.

As for me, I threw God out with the Bible-belt bathwater when I was a kid, and soon began to explore the mysteries of life and the concepts of truth through reading, thinking, writing and listening to my own inner realms. Over the years I received many bits and clues along the way about truth and its seemingly endless varieties of expression. But I hit a wall in my understanding until a remarkable series of events catapulted me into a personal experience of Christic Presence which introduced me to love – a love that was beyond anything I had ever experienced. In one fell-swoop moment my heart was "broken open," and I began what would be, and is still, an ongoing spiritual journey into the greater depths and more whole truths that only love can yield.

The quest to seek and find love and truth has had me exploring a number of traditions for many years now. It seems that we are each truly met in whatever vocabulary and path we choose as we pursue our universal but individually-orchestrated search for Self, meaning and purpose, connection with others and communion with the Divine. Because of our diversities, "all roads lead home" – and we are met on the path, or pathlessness, that most facilitates our soul development and purpose in humanity. Every person, path and way, every dogma and tradition, holds a unique truth-piece of the cosmic puzzle. This suggests, as the Angel wisdoms say, that in order to get the full "Bigger Picture" of the Divine, Creation, the cosmos and our place within it, we need to welcome the pieces everyone else holds as well.

The only way we can do that is through a sense of unity, love and the other profound resources of our hearts, which include compassion, intuition, wisdom and understanding. Ultimately, it is only through Love that we may discern the whole Truth, for Love activates the hologram of the Divine I AM which we carry within our own souls. This is why working with the "angles" of Divine Light is so powerful for us – because they are gifts of the Divine Heart given to awaken and amplify our soul-light within our sacred human hearts, where we may come within to remember our true nature.

Return to Unity

To reprise from Volume 4, **underneath our differences is a sameness of heart that allows us to come into unity from the inside, even while we are separate and diverse beings on the "outside**." We struggle with the concepts of separation and unity between us, as if unity is the more spiritually desirable concept, and separation an illusion – which some spiritual vocabularies suggest. However, the Angel Wisdoms tell us that both separation and unity are sacred, necessary and possible on Earth. For even while we exist in physical separateness here for the expansion of Divine diversity within human diversity of form and expression – at any moment we can return to unity and the "Garden of Eden" that is the heart of God by returning to the sameness of heart within, between and among us each and all.

Simply, though profoundly, we are the many which express the One that is at the heart and soul of who we are. As such, here we all are on the Divine Tree of our shared origin, each of us angling into the light and catching wind with all our own unique ways and wonders. Yet not only do we lose sight of the Tree and forget the trunk and roots that sustain us – we often treat the other leaves on the Tree not as our brothers and sisters, but our distant poor relations and even our enemies. In the greater reality beyond and despite our forgetting, however, not only is the Tree sustaining all of us, but it takes all of us to express the fullness of the Tree's own potential. Just as it also takes all of us to bring the totality of life-giving light that the Tree's roots need in order to keep sustaining us. For truly, and ultimately, we cannot individually thrive on Earth unless we all thrive.

The Wisdom of CAHETEL (Divine Blessings) elaborates beautifully on living the blessings of both diversity and unity:

The birth of otherness from the One, and a third from two, are the great cosmic blessings of creation and regeneration that continually expand life. How do you participate in and multiply these Divine blessings? By being a blessing to each other – through mutual companionship, kindness, giving and receiving. By being each other's soft landings, helping hands and comforting shoulders. By extending leeway, latitude and non-judgment. Through seeing more than meets the eye by looking with your heart. By seeing your diversity as the contrast that inspires you to define and fine-tune your own uniqueness. By seeing your sameness of heart and the spirit of love and life that dwells within each of you and is expressed outwardly so uniquely. By realizing that the animals, trees and other flora are your friends, teachers and co-creators, and that all things of the Earth are alive and sentient beings, affected by everything you think, feel and do.

Someday we will be enlightened enough to not only tolerate our differences, but embrace them – even be curious and delighted about them, as the Divine Itself is and as we are as children before we become *adulterated.* And we will realize how vital for our continuation and thriving are our beautiful varieties of being and doing, as well as our unity, at every level of life.

The World's Ills: Responsibility vs. Blame

The Angel Wisdoms suggest to us again and again to look at the negative happenings in both our personal lives and world events not as how terrible our lives are or the world is – but rather as indications, or symptoms, of where healing is needed. Things that stay hidden, denied or suppressed do not get healed. They just fester and build momentum until one day they explode from some kind of "last straw" stressor. And though we are shocked and horrified, closer examination reveals that the signs were there – and yet eyes were looking away or hands were wringing in frustration and a sense of helplessness for any way to cure the problem.

Most of us want to focus on the positive aspects and potentials of life, naturally so. However, life in time expresses through the prism of duality – in which our experiences can be both "uni-versal" and "inverse," which suggest to see the One and *not* see the One, i.e., light and shadow. These give us the contrast that can stimulate growth and expansion, and thus saying yes to life itself means saying yes to both. Saying yes to the presence of the darker aspects means being willing to play the hand life deals us by using our courage and creativity to turn whatever happens into something more light-and-life-affirming.

The shadows are painful, however, and so we have a tendency to want to sweep seemingly unresolvable problems under the rug, especially if they don't affect us or our loved ones directly. And if our loved ones are involved, and everything we've done to help still isn't working and we don't know what else to do, we get battle weary and feelings of fatigue and defeat set in. This particularly applies in cases of mental disturbance, post-traumatic stress, drug and alcohol addiction and such. Most of us, and many of our communities, are not equipped to attend to the complexities of individuals with deep-seeded issues such as these. But if left unattended, as we have seen, sometimes families and communities can suffer horrific violence at the hands of those very people, which turns the problem of an individual into a community problem – which from the perspective of our underlying unity was a community issue in the first place.

Sometimes we don't know what to do or how to help because we get caught up in blame of self or others. But blame is never an answer or a resolution – in fact it's more of a blinder or paralyzer. The Wisdom of MANAKEL (Knowledge of Good and Evil) talks about this need to blame:

> *Often after negative events in your world there is much time and effort spent on trying to determine who's to blame rather than who will step up to help course-correct – as if being part of the solution will somehow admit to blame for the problem. We tell you this – there is never one cause of any 'bad act.' The need to narrow the field of blame and hold someone accountable is often driven by the need to 'put an end to the matter' and restore some sense of safety and absolution to everyone else.*

From the perspective of the Angel Wisdoms, rather than trying to affix blame – as if that will let the rest of us off the hook – our real task is to realize our collective responsibility for what goes on in our world. Through the generations of sowing and reaping, we see only the current transgressions – but the truth is that rarely can causality be attributed to only one particular person, group or event today, or in the yesterdays of the generations. The Wisdom for HAZIEL (Divine Mercy and Forgiveness) talks about this:

> *In a perceived wrongdoing by any person or group, it is very common with the passing of time, and even generations, to lose sight of when the 'worm first burrowed into the apple.' One act begets another and that begets another, and so on and on – because in the polarities of physical life, for every action there is a reaction, as you say. The cure for this is not more blame, judgment, punishment, or 'an eye for an eye' vengeance, because these only perpetuate more of the same. The cure is to interrupt the cycles of hurt with love, mercy, compassion and mutual responsibility.*

IMAMIAH (Expiation of Errors) reiterates:

> *It is not blame you are asked to acknowledge, but responsibility. It does not matter whether the fault was on the part of 'the chicken or the egg.' What matters is that the chicken and the egg are in it together, and both of them need each other.*

And so, even though you or I personally may not have been a direct accomplice in a particular event – or done anything in our lives to cause hurt to another or add to the world's ills (!) – by virtue of our existence and our collective responsibility for a humane world, we must each and all step up in ways that we can in order to contribute to the kind of world we want to live in.

Responsibility for our rights and privileges. We've all heard the saying, "to whom much is given, much is expected." Heart-and-mindfulness about how we exercise our rights and privileges as citizens of our communities and nations is vital to our peaceful co-existence. While working on Volume 5, the *Charlie Hebdo* satirical magazine was attacked by gunmen in Paris evidently because of their numerous depictions of the prophet Muhammad in their magazine. Of course, the whole world was horrified at this blatant act of terrorism against civilians and artists which took so many lives and also offended the 'right of free speech.'

Uncannily, that day of January 7 corresponded to the Angel HAIYAEL, for Divine Warrior and Weaponry. What an incredible display of the inversion of this light-energy! As I listened to the news coverage, and all the free-speech commentary, two things came up in the Angelic communications: *"just because you can doesn't always mean you should"* – and – *"for deeper cause, look to the generations of disenfranchisement among the tribes and nations."* The first is about using our rights and privileges with respect, and the second is about sowing and reaping and how the universe is always seeking balance. Thus what is taken will ultimately be taken back – even generations later.

In the days that followed the Paris attack, these very topics began to be debated by European journalists and thought leaders, and the internet is now full of editorial articles looking at *Charlie Hebdo* and other such terror attacks and tragedies from every angle. In perusing some of the editorials, several in particular stood out to me, the first of which I think is problematic.

Reverend Michael Heath:

> Given the global village that we inhabit, we need to get used to being offended and stop being so outraged when something we hold dear is challenged.

(www.syracuse.com/opinion/index.ssf/2015/01/rethinking_whats_offensive_in_a_post-charlie_hebdo_world_commentary.html)

While I agree with this in theory, I think it's an ideal that appeals to the educated, and even privileged, and neglects the "tinderbox" atmosphere of our world in which so many people are on the edge of what they can tolerate in terms of continual disenfranchisement. Tess Finch Lees of www.independent.co.uk addressed this in her editorial, saying:

> Mockery is a weapon to be aimed at the powerful, not at the marginalised and disenfranchised. ...'Free speech' is a privilege accessible to those who can afford it.

(www.independent.co.uk/voices/comment/charlie-hebdo-mockery-is-a-weapon-to-be-aimed-at-the-powerful-not-at-the-marginalised-and-disenfranchised-9977827.html)

A thoughtful editorial was written by Anne-Marie Slaughter, President and CEO of the New America Foundation, a Professor Emerita at Princeton University and a member of the World Economic Forum Global Agenda. While she supports the right of free speech, she also felt that "support of the principle does not demand endorsement of the practice."

> In the case of *Charlie Hebdo*, the question is whether depictions of the Prophet Muhammad are likely to foster the kinds of debate and behavior that are compatible with the coexistence of Muslims, Christians, Jews, other believers, and atheists in a society that upholds the freedom of worship and expression. All human beings are entitled to hold something – a place, an idea, an image – sacred. Desecrating a shrine, defacing a cross, or, in the US, burning a flag, is an aggressive and insulting act, one that causes real pain for believers. It may incite a conversation, but it does so from a position of profound disrespect. [Emphasis added]

(www.project-syndicate.org/commentary/charlie-hebdo-rights-wrongs-by-anne-marie-slaughter-2015-01#KUebkfY1JOawyrRZ.99)

As I was on my way to a café to have a late lunch and finish writing this section, I heard on the car radio that there had been an attack against a Copenhagen café where a meeting was taking place about free speech and blasphemy in the arts. The attack was thought to be directed particularly at the Swedish artist Lars Vilks. Mr. Vilks, in a brief interview with a journalist admitted to often "insulting" Islam and the prophet Muhammad. The journalist asked him if it wasn't arrogance to disrespect the religion of those who take their religion very seriously. His answer was, "nobody loves the truth, but someone's got to speak it." While that may sound artistically and philosophically noble – it struck me in another way. He used the term "*the* truth." But might we not say that his, or anyone's truth is relative, and thus only **a** truth, **their** truth, **my** truth or **yours** – not **THE** truth? The commentators went on to discuss the roles of artists in our societies to sometimes provoke thought and discussion, and one said, "yes, free speech is important to freedom and a democratic society – but if you shout 'fire' in a crowded theater [as a joke], you will likely be arrested."

So the issue then widens to the question of using our rights responsibly. Just because we have "the right to offend" as one New Yorker staff writer defended, doesn't mean we should. Just because free speech gives us the right to bully, mock, curse, defame, disrespect and spew out verbally violent missiles of hurt and hate, doesn't mean we should. In many ways it's the same issue as the right to bear arms – just because we can doesn't mean we should – nor does it mean that we should be shooting each other with them. So how then should we be governed in the exercise of our rights? When do we cross the line from the beneficent purposes intended when those rights were first legislated to becoming a license to cause harm?

We often use the phrase in our everyday lives, "too much of a good thing" when we are feeling the effects of over-indulgence. Too much of anything can create imbalance, distortion and misuse. The global conversation about rights and privileges, including artistic rights, is now exploring the need for more discernment, i.e., heart-and-mindfulness about what we create with our creations. Do we want to bring more light to the world, or darken the shadows? While exposing the "dark" helps to bring it into the light where it can be healed, can we not find ways to do it without inciting more harm?

"*If the pen is to be mightier than the sword,*" the Wisdom of DANIEL (Eloquence) says, "*then the pen must do what the sword cannot.*" The true "weapons of mass creation," as one post-*Charlie Hebdo* artist put it, are not weapons at all – but love, compassion, forgiveness and respect – and we must consider that any truth expressed without the greater sensibilities of these is only part-truth. Through the ages, it has always been a part-truth, in the guise of an "only truth," that divides and incites bias, hate and hurt.

As the Angelic light-energies and all that is Divine tell us, only love can take all the pieces of truth that each of us hold and put them together. Only love can create something more powerful than an "only truth:" a WHOLE truth – born from love, discovered in love and carried out in love between and among us. Jesus, St. Francis, Buddha, Ghandi, Mother Teresa and so many more used their lives to show us this. We must find the sameness of heart beneath our differences so that we can come to embrace this love-and-life-affirming truth held deep within us: "*The only battle worth winning is the one that cannot be fought.*"

The community and global impact of personal pain. While the Angel Wisdoms continually illuminate the power we have as individuals to help heal the world, there is also of course the inversion of that – the possibility for individuals who are hurting and desperate to strike out at the world. These are individuals living among us – someone we might think is a little odd, or someone who acts perfectly normal. They are the pointers to the issues we try to ignore or bury in our societies. Their victims might be particular people or cultures they blame for their problems or for some particular offense, or random strangers who represent "the world" that denies them opportunity or belonging. But whether these tragedies are about severe mental illness or emotional issues, domestic abuse, anger, revenge, disenfranchisement, alignment with skewed ideologies, or other things, "lone-gunman" violence is hard to predict or prevent. And these are who terrorist groups are recruiting and exploiting, just for that reason.

A couple days after the Copenhagen attack, I glanced at the news to see a discussion with John Miller, head of New York's intelligence and counter-terrorism unit, as he summarized the challenge in dealing with the "lone wolf" type of attacker:

> These individuals self-radicalize not always because of an ideology, but because they are failing in the life they have. A militant or terrorist group promises valor, belonging and empowerment – valor for one who feels like a nobody and needs recognition…belonging for one who feels like an outcast… empowerment for the disenfranchised.

An editorial at www.theguardian.com echoed this:

> Sometimes such radicalism becomes a perverse refuge in a quest for identity and self-affirmation.

www.theguardian.com/commentisfree/2015/jan/08/guardian-view-response-terror-attack-charlie-hebdo-crime-act-war

Miller went so far to say that "governments can't fight this kind of enemy...the task is to get the local communities to reach individuals who are susceptible to this" before they escalate.

These statements echo the messages about disenfranchisement in the Daily Wisdoms. An increasing number of violent situations involve individuals who are reacting in extreme ways against a society in which they feel they have no place. But it makes complete spiritual sense that those who are hurting to the extent that they must strike out at others should all now be "coming out of the woodwork" to let us know that our global crises must be addressed closer to home, in our own families and communities. The "walking wounded" among us are not going to go away by ignoring them. If our power truly is in the collectives of individuals, then we have to provide ways for the hurting ones among us to get the help they need, and we must stop marginalizing and disempowering each other into conditions of deprivation, poverty and alienation.

As individuals, we can pay more attention to what's happening with our friends and families. We can befriend our neighbors, and perhaps be part of local policy-making and helping initiatives. One of the most powerful things we can do at local levels is to rehabilitate how policing is done in our communities so that police officers might be regarded as allies instead of enemies. (Imagine if communities would have real input into how they are policed!) I recently saw an article about how the 2007 revamping of police protocols and practices in Richmond, California – a town that was once #9 in the nation in reported crimes – reduced crime about 66% from 2007 to 2014, with no fatal shootings, and only one officer-involved shooting a year. The new police chief got rid of the "bad apples" in the department, stopped street harassments and practices like "stop and frisk," and assigned officers to regular beats so that neighborhoods could come to know them and form more trusting relationships. The department also developed a program in which potential offenders were identified and given a mentor and $300-$1000 a month (via private donors) to help get them into programs and opportunities for education and work.

Again, the key is awareness, as well as attitude. We must learn to look at everyone in our communities as "us" – not "us and them" – because our attitudes are not going to protect us. Rather it is those very attitudes, along with the fear, denial and elitism that form them, which are endangering all of us.

The "good news," according to the Angel Wisdoms, is that all the volatile issues in our world are accelerated opportunities for healing if we address them. Thus, the Wisdom of HAIYAEL encourages us:

> *I tell you as HAIYAEL that just as those who visit your upper atmospheres can see the blanket of Earth-dweller lights twinkling through the dark, we of the cosmic realms see the inner soul-lights of all humanity radiating from time into eternity. And we tell you that however much darkness may seem to be rampant upon the Earth, it is nothing compared to your combined light. Although it may appear that there are more and more beings in your world warring against each other, there are also more than ever before who are 'leaning into' the light of love, compassion, peace and harmony.*
>
> *...And so, we say – do not lose heart with your world – because your Earth, and your heart, are where love has come to put down roots, and the truth is that in the end, as in the beginning, 'love is all there is.'*

Daily Life with the 72 Angels

In my research, writings and mystical work with the 72 Angels and Kabbalah cosmology, the big change-of-paradigm message has been to reunite the Divine and the human – to stop thinking of God as somewhere out or up there, separate, unknowable and ever judging us from afar. These notions are human constructs that were fed to us centuries ago, which we have continued to be susceptible to because of our need to feel that there is something "greater" and "better" than us that will protect us from ourselves and help to make sense of this crazy world. Because of this notion of a separate God – as well as the perpetuated concept of original sin that has made humanity feel separate and never quite "good enough" – the potential and powerful fullness of our human experience has been denied us. In our search for "salvation," we must come to realize that it is the Divine *within* us that will save us, for our own souls are made of that very greater and better stuff that is within, among and all around us. To my understanding, this is one of the revelations that Jesus came to convey through the example of his own life and his words – "these things I do, you can do and more...the Kingdom of Heaven is within," etc. – and through the quickening of the Christic Spirit of Divine Love and Compassion within and among us.

I was originally led to the 72 Angels tradition because it seemed to explain many of the Christic mysteries that church dogma has guarded over the centuries as precepts of faith. My own spiritual awakening came through mystical Christic experiences that involved loving and compassion events of deep personal resonance. In being led to the Kabbalah some years after having delved deeply into the Bible, I realized, of course, that Jesus was Jewish, not Christian, and he would have been steeped in the Jewish mysteries during his mysterious education in the temples where he was said to have displayed remarkable understanding – not to mention other likely wisdoms and influences during his travels in the "missing years."

Thus, in never having been properly indoctrinated by any church or doctrine, I was prompted inwardly to hear and approach all with an open heart and mind. I saw that at the heart of the Kabbalah's Angelic tradition were the same profound mysteries of love, compassion, the grace of transformation and the awakening of the Divine within the human that are found in the innermost, non-dogmatic aspects of the Christic mysteries.

I realize now that I had never been drawn to popular angelogy because it somehow still kept the Divine outside of us. I understand the need to relate to and rely on an outer Other, but the deeper mysteries call us into relationship with the inner Other first, and then to relationship with the inner Other of outer others – if you get my drift! Essentially, seeing God within ourselves and in each other and every thing and being. Thus, I was ultimately led away from the stereotypical depictions and concepts of Angels. Instead they were shown to me as refracted "angles" of the Divine Light and Being – emanations of the Divine Itself that revealed the diversity within its Oneness.

This is in keeping with what certain ancient Judeo-Christian literatures call "Angels of the Presence...which came forth on the first day," not as created beings, but as emanations that represent the faces of God, as God Itself. Thus, as angles, aspects and qualities of the Divine Oneness-Light, the 72 Angels are said to dwell within and among us as sentient presences to awaken and amplify awareness of our inner Divine nature that is our soul-light. Furthermore, because the Divine is angelically pervasive in our humanity, we must realize that when we invoke an Angel, we are actually calling upon a particular light-quality of the Divine *that is already within us* to quicken and expand within our own *awareness*.

This is akin to the way aboriginal and native tribes see and relate with the "Great Spirit" through Its diverse manifestations and expressions as, for example, the light of the sun, the moon and stars, the winds and rains, the Earth and her waters – and the spirit found within the animals and plants and every created thing and being. Shamanism, indeed, represents the mystical means by which the human might commune and align with these particular aspects and attributes of the Great Spirit that are revealed in the natural world. This is also akin to the Hindu pantheon of gods, which each represent an aspect of the one Great Brahman who is absolute "creator and enjoyer of all creation." Thus, through each "god," the worshipper may commune with a diverse and particular attribute of the One.

Being able to draw on aspects of the Divine that pertain particularly to our specific challenges and potentials gives us a sense that we are not alone here – because the Divine is responsive to us and our needs in a way that feels personal. Indeed, at the mystical heart of so many traditions is this mystery: that the Divine presence is conscious within our own consciousness – and the more awake and aware we are, the more we may experience the Divine within us as a living breathing presence living through, and as, us, creating our life experience with us.

Thus, my own journey of bringing forth the Angelic Wisdoms, and the experiences of others working with them as a daily practice, are about the steady cultivation of **awareness** and the subtle, but profound, transformations that take place because of the daily and moment-to-moment renewal of awareness. Each day's message puts in our hearts and minds the particular quality and potential of the day's Angel, or "angle" of light, which palpitates our awareness of that quality through our encounters, conversations and events, giving us opportunities to more heartfully address whatever comes up with empathy, compassion and wisdom.

One woman detailed very colorfully how her relationship to television news programs had changed:

> My habit for ages has been to start the day watching the news. I figured out that everyone had an agenda, so I watched them all – Fox, CNN, MSNBC, BBC, Glenn Beck, etc. – trying to get to the facts, somewhere in the middle. It was like a drug. The only thing I accomplished was getting thoroughly pissed off every day, because no one tells the facts without embellishment, and I still didn't know for sure what was going on. So, I started doing the daily wisdoms every morning instead, and gradually refocused on

> my own stuff, through the lens of the readings. A lot of the change involves figuring out what MY beliefs are (an ongoing challenge), and how that relates to what's going on in the rest of the world. Amazing how much easier it is to get perspective when I get back to me! Now I start the day in a much more peaceful frame of mind and don't stay furious all the time. Plus, I'm sending out more smiles.

Another woman wrote that she and her husband, who both work with the Wisdoms, experience that on many days "the Angel offers what [we] need to hear precisely when we need to hear it. We feel so completely companioned and in full awareness of the Angel presence..."

Some additional experiences with the Wisdoms:

> The journey with the 'dailies' has been profound for me – I love them!! I read first in the morning and review at night...often taking a quick look at the next day's Angel to know what energy I'll be sleeping with after midnight. I really like this practice especially if I'm feeling tender. ...I find great strength and comfort in certain passages, and in all ways the dailies richly inform my living...

> I have found that once started, the conversation with the Angels is ongoing and has many different expressions...I am particularly amazed how the coincidences that happen which are connected to the day's Angel are reminders for me to be aware and present, and even to handle things differently than I might have.

> I recognize that Angelic assistance is near, constant and available...thus I am able to live in gratitude with ease... feeling hopeful, balanced, centered and protected. The daily wisdoms give me focus and awareness of what may present itself in my practice of reflexology and 'pedi-curing' for the day. My goal: to feel the angelic love, then give it to others during my day, and hopefully evolve to 'be' love.

> I use the wisdoms to frame my daily thoughts and actions, usually starting with reading the day's wisdom first thing in the morning. As my day progresses, I often recognize when that day's heart angel is communicating with me via other people in conversation or experience; and since I set my awareness, I am better able to recognize in a deeper way how the communication is significant for my own growth and understanding.

With everyone I've heard from, a common thread is the power of repetition to accumulate and deepen awareness. Even for myself in the co-creating of the Wisdoms, I would sometimes hear a concept over and over, said in different ways, and still not get the important gist of it for weeks or even months. Or if I did get it, it wouldn't sink in until maybe the 10th time I heard it! The repetition of the same information – as in the same lesson over and over – allows things to be presented to us from different angles in different scenarios and vocabularies until one day the light finally dawns!

In order to help refresh the importance of daily awareness in working with the Angels, this next section is a reprise from previous volumes, with some additional details.

Ongoing Work and Play with the Angels

There is always so much more to see than we are looking at, so much more to feel than we are reaching for, so much more to know than what has been handed down to us by others. As the Daily Wisdoms help to increase awareness of our magnificent inner resources, the soul-voice within our hearts and our Angelic support system amplify the Divine within all the inner and outer parts of our human beingness. As we begin to experience the Angels and ourselves in this light, we see the greater potential of our own being, each other and all of life.

In the growing of our daily Angelic awareness, there is less space within us for doubts, fears, guilt, shame and old hurts, and more room for the truth of who we are and the self-love that enables us to truly love others. Looking through our "Angel-eyes," we see their messages and gifts waiting in the wings of every moment, encounter, conversation and coincidence. Our daily lives become full of signs, wonders, symbols and clues to unlock the meanings and purposes of our gifts, opportunities and challenges.

Through the 72 Angels we come to understand that we each exist as a uniqueness of being and potential within the Divine Oneness, and the Divine Oneness exists within us in order to enhance the qualities and powers of our humanity. Thus both the Divine and the human get to experience and co-create life as only each of us can live it through Divine-Human beingness.

Thus, when we welcome the Angels as *angles*, or qualities, of Divine Light – we are not asking them to come to us from "Above." What we are doing is inviting our awareness to awaken and see that they are already here within and around and among us. By welcoming them, we acknowledge their presence and our willingness to engage their Divine magnificence shimmering within us as the potential of our own magnificence. Thus we might become the true and fulfilled Divine-Human beings we are here to be and thereby offer the greater treasure of ourselves to the healing and fulfillment of our world.

Angelic alchemy. And so, as in the Divine-Human mysteries of many spiritual paths and vocabularies, we are called to three things in our practice with the Angels: **ask**, **receive** and **become** – which echoes the Biblical words attributed to Jesus of how to access our Divine power. This ongoing 3-step "Divine-alchemy" can ultimately transform our base *mettle* into the spiritual gold of one who has realized the love and truth of who we are, as the Divine Itself dwelling within us and as us. These steps can be done in meditation or prayer with the day's Angel and also used to focus attention and awareness for everything we encounter during our day.

Remember as you do this that you are working with specific aspects and energies of the Divine, as angles of the Divine Light That It is – not separate created beings.

1. **Ask** (Invoke) – Pray/chant/speak the Angel's name, open your heart and invite its presence to expand within you.

2. **Receive** (Imbibe) – Breathe in, listen, meditate upon and allow the Angel's essence and energy to expand within your heart and being.

3. **Become** (Embody) – Absorb, digest and assimilate the Angel's qualities into the very belly of your beingness so that your awareness and action come into harmony (as in 'walking the talk').

Becoming aware and present with the Angels is meant to prompt you to engage with your own within as the Divine Light that shimmers in, and as, your own soul, and which is illuminated in your heart as your personal truth. Thus, follow the inner prompts from that not so still, not so small voice in your heart as the voice of an Angel within, in unison with and amplification of your own soul and its purposes. Slowly, or even epiphanously, the effects will become cumulative and life-transforming.

I suggest to create some quiet time for a few moments every day to read and contemplate the day's Angel-wisdom. Remember that the message is meant to speak to your heart, and note the parts that resonate with you. As you go through your day notice what is echoed in conversations and encounters, and where you can use the qualities of that day's Angel to be more heartful with yourself, your work and others. Pay attention to the moments that trigger a feeling or resonance, which will indicate a timely relevance to you. Begin to see the connections between you and everything and everyone which are sometimes signaled by coincidence and unexpected encounters. **For every question you have and whatever truth you seek, consider that the answer is love – and look to what love is calling you to in that moment**.

The Seasons of Our Lives

The Angels tell us that this plane of existence is NOT an illusion. What is an illusion is to think that this world's reality, or our own outer beingness, is *all* there is. This world is a particular context of time, space and place for the Divine and human to "join forces" in order to be and do things that can't be done anywhere else in the universe! But because of the lower vibrational density here that allows the physical formation of matter, we easily lose touch with our lighter, ethereal origins and inner natures.

As the Angel Wisdoms say, we are like leaves so far out on our branches that we forget the source that supports us, the roots that sustain us, and the heart-sap that nourishes us. We're each just out there waving in the wind, catching the light from all our different angles and changing colors with the seasons of our being and doing, feeling and thinking. Nevertheless, for all our forgetting, we are not forgotten by the Source itself as we are sustained for all our days here. And then the day comes when like the leaf, our forms fall and what we leave behind becomes nutrients for those who come after us. No longer contained and constricted in form, our essence is freed to experience that, however magnificent it was to be a physical being, we are now, and once again, far more than we were as physical forms. For our greater life – our essential life – is eternal.

The greatest opportunity of our humanity, however, is to experience this eternal within us while we are still physical beings so that our experience of living might be truly 'larger than life!'

We can learn so much from nature about being both form and essence. Thus, the Angels' Daily Wisdoms follow the flow and energies of the seasons expressed in the natural world and also in our own lives. Just as with the Divine and the entire cosmos since the first "moments" of emanation and differentiation of the One into the many of Creation, everything and everyone is birthed and moves through life not only seasonally, but daily, through cycles of ebb and flow in the context of **relationship**. When we really begin to see how our lives cycle, and that each of us have our own particular cadence as we move into and through each cycle, we appreciate that our lives are not random – but relative and responsive to the smallest and grandest ripples in our personal, global and universal contexts of living, loving, being and doing.

The 72 Angels' yearly cycle begins March 21, corresponding to our relationship with the Divine and our soul's cosmic birth, from which all else emerges. The 72 Angels in their daily heart dominion cycle five times a year (72 x 5 + some overlapping days = 365):

Spring ~ 3/21–6/2: Relationship with the Divine. The newborn green of Spring symbolizes our cosmic birth and what the soul regards as our primary relationship with the Divine Itself as our origin. Just as with the Spring rebirth of many forms of Creation in the natural world, we too experience the quickening and joy of new beingness and awakening to the world in fresh ways as we sprout new beginnings and creations that have been gestating within us during the Winter.

Summer ~ 6/3–8/16: Relationship with Self. This is a time of exploration and celebration of ourselves through self-love, gladness, the lighterness of being, living, loving and playing in the present and the flowering and ripening of our unique potentials.

Fall ~ 8/17–10/29: Relationship with Work and Purpose. This is the season for harvesting the fruits of our summer and scattering new seeds as we get back to work after vacations and times of fun and relaxation. While outer forms begin to fall away, we begin a deeper exploration into meaning and purpose as we continue to cultivate our individuation through new ideas, projects and collaborations.

The "Holy-days" of Late Fall/Early Winter ~ 10/30–1/8: Relationship with Others. Here the Angels bring us to heart-and-mindfulness in our interpersonal relatings at the time of year when we gather with loved ones and those in our immediate circles to celebrate the holidays and holy days of the season. In coming together with those who matter most, where the need for forgiveness and healing is often most apparent, we see the opportunity through self-transformation to transform and enliven our relationships.

Winter ~ 1/9–3/20: Relationship with community and the world. In this last volume, the 72 Angels bring the five Angelic cycles of the year to completion. Here the Wisdoms address how we each bring our unique self, individuation, purposes and interpersonal relatings to our communities and the collective consciousness of the world, including the Earth. From the gestation and nurturing of our own withins during the dormancy of winter's inwardness, new ideas, wisdoms and ways soon begin to sprout for a renewed and even reborn self that we may bring to the awakening world.

As previously mentioned, the seasonal references in the Angel wisdoms are reversed for those in the southern hemisphere, and less dramatic for those who live closer to the equator. However, like the play of the microcosmic within the macrocosmic at every level of life, within every season are "sub-seasons" that mirror all the seasons in one – from new beginnings, growth, harvest, endings and gestational transition to rebirth in the next season. Thus, if the seasons for you are reversed, I suggest that in the context of using the Daily Wisdoms you may either work with the symbolism of the sub-seasons or use the volumes in a different order – but remembering that all our relatings and doings start with our relationship to the Divine.

Nurturing the Seeds of the Winter

Winter, or any time of seeming dormancy or inwardness, is often when the least amount of activity seems to be happening on the outside, as profound change is happening on the inside. Drawn within to the realms of spirit, thought, emotion and inner ruminations, we may be more reserved outwardly. As we "recuperate" from the holidays and try to get back to our regular routines and schedules – perhaps along with some renewed resolutions for health and exercise – we are thinking about what we want to make of the new year in a way that is more than just ticking off our to-do lists. We may contemplate who we are, where we've been, where we want to go and how we might bring greater meaning and purpose into our endeavors.

Interestingly, this gestative inwardness, in which new thoughts and ideas are taking shape within us, mirrors our time in the womb, when our own human forms are taking shape from a tiny fertilized "seed" invisible to the human eye. We have this insistence upon "the need to see in order to believe" – but so much of life is seeded by the unseen! Thoughts, ideas, feelings and cross-pollinations between two – these are all seeds of creation that bring something new from an invisible seeming no-thing. And every living thing, for the most part, has the power to re-seed when it reaches maturation. How beautifully we mirror what Kabbalists call "the first swirlings" of an unknowable Divine "No-thingness" as it Its energies began to stir into what would become the diverse creations of the Universe.

Just as our own thoughts, feelings and actions are the seeds of our own becoming, we are seeding our world every day, all day long, with the emissions of our individuality through words, attitudes and actions at every level unto others. Thus, the Wisdoms say, each individual is a unique Divinely-endowed seed in the potential full and diverse flowering of humanity. How we blossom in our own lives determines the hues we bring to the rest of humanity. Blessedly for us, and the world, we have every new day to cultivate new ways of being and blossoming anew, as the first of the 72 Angels, VEHUIAH, encourages:

> *Let the dawning of new light be warm and gentle among you, encouraging the seeding of ideas in a co-creative atmosphere where each contribution is a gift that helps the whole to increase information, knowledge and wisdom as you collaborate on your goal. Even be willing to forego 'how it was always done' in order to create new ways and means that will better serve the needs of your community and world as it is now. Let the past not imprison the present, but be a teacher and inspirer of the future.*

The Daily Wisdoms

The 72 Angels' Days of Heart Support

In case you did not start the *Book of Days* series with the first four volumes, repeated here are the various associations accompanying the Daily Angel Wisdoms which relate to the Angel's position on the Tree of Life, and also give clues to its nature: the Sephira of the Tree in which the Angel resides, its overlighting Archangel, astrological and date associations and more.

Sephirot Pages: These introduce the Sephira (vessel or sphere) in which each group (choir) of eight Angels reside on the Tree of Life, as well as the qualities and functions of the overlighting Archangel.

Date: The current day of the Angel's expression and support through our heart plane is bolded; the other dates represent its four other "heart-days" of influence and support during the year. Since it is helpful to be aware of your Heart Angel not only on your birthday, but also its other four days of influence, you may want to mark your personal calendar with all five days. Note also that the yearly cycle for the 72 Angels begins March 21, the time of the Spring Equinox, which is the beginning of "Nissan," the first month of the year in the Jewish calendar. In my research I also ran across an obscure variant in the date attributions of the Angelic cycles, but the one used in all the *Birth Angels* materials is the cycle that the 12th-15th century school of Isaac the Blind and his followers and fellow Kabbalists were working with throughout the centuries. (See Appendix II for more info.)

An Angel's full day of influence goes from 12:00 am midnight to 12:00 am midnight, 24 hours later (00:00-24:00 in Europe, etc.). A few of the Angels' days overlap to support a total of 365 days. In a leap year of 366 days, the Angel for February 28 also governs the 29th. The "am" designation always goes from 12:00 am midnight to 12:00 pm noon (00:00-12), and the "pm" from 12:00 pm noon to

12:00 am midnight (12:00-24:00). Of course, 12:00 is a cusp minute for both day and night. An Angel that governs for a day and a half, for example, 4/16 + 17 am, would span from 12:00 am midnight as the 15th passes to the 16th, to 12:00 pm noon on the 17th (midnight to midnight to noon) (00:00-24:00-12:00).

Note: Kabbalists have historically worked with the 72 Angels through their correspondences to the Zodiacal degrees totaling 360, the circumference of a circle. Ultimately a correspondence of degrees to actual days was needed in order to accommodate our 365-day calendar, which meant that a few of the Angelic Energies would be attributed to more than one day. Because the degrees to days correspondences change slightly every year, it can be helpful to be aware of the Angelic Energy that comes before and after each of your Birth Angels or the one you are working with at a particular date or time, and notice if you feel more resonant with one more than another. (Thanks to Tristan Llop, son of Kabaleb, for explaining this to me!) Ultimately our lives are about what we do with the energies that present themselves to us – for we have the innate power to use everything that comes our way as an ally.

The Angel's number and name: The number for each Angel represents the order of its position on the Tree of Life and its degrees of correspondence to the Zodiacal wheel of time – and if you study astrology and numerology these may give additional insight into both the Angels and the stars. The Angel's name is a transliteration of its Hebrew name. The origin of the names is from what the Kabbalah refers to as the 72 "Intelligences" or "Names of God" as the "Shem HaMephorash,"), which are each composed of a three-letter combination derived from a "decoding" of Exodus 14:19-21 in Hebrew. While vowels were originally left out of the Angels' Hebrew Names to create ambiguity in order to protect the sacred Names of God, in later centuries the "niqqud" (vowel marks) were added to help with pronunciation. Each Angel's name ends in either "IAH" or "EL," denoting that the name is a Name and Quality of God. I have found in some Kabbalah literature that IAH represents the feminine aspect and EL the masculine, representing the inherent masculine-feminine unity within the Divine which is expressed in duality as polarities, as all manifestations of life.

You will notice if you consult other sources through the ages that the spellings of the Angels' names vary greatly. This is the result of varied dialects and permutations in the Hebrew language and its transliterations through centuries of dispersion of the Jewish people into different cultures and sects. I have done extensive research on this, but in the end have chosen to follow most of the spellings that the works of Kabaleb put forth based on his extensive research of prominent medieval and Renaissance Kabbalists working with this system. (See Appendix II herein for details.)

Pronunciation guide: This is given to help with saying or chanting the Angel's name aloud in meditation or prayer as you invite the Angel's energies to expand within you. All the names are emphasized (shown in ALL CAPS) on the last syllable, IAH or EL, to show that the name is a quality and aspect of God. Names with more than two syllables have two accented syllables, as in "Neh-MA-mee-YAH." Kabbalah creation cosmology regards the sounds and forms of the Hebrew letters as having the power to transmit Divine Energies and even bring forth new life. This is akin to the use of the word "Om" and Sanskrit chants to invoke the Divine within.

Angel's quality/function and G/R/S designation: This represents the Divine attribute which the Angel embodies and amplifies within you, and whether the attribute is expressed outwardly (G, for "Going out" from the Divine and down the Tree of Life toward manifestation), inwardly (R for "Returning" back up the Tree to the Divine through ascending consciousness), or in a state of equilibrium which can be expressed outwardly or inwardly (S for Stabilized).

The qualities of the Angels seem to have been attributed beyond the literal meanings of their Hebrew letters to reflect their astrological associations, as well as revelations received by those working with the Angelic Energies through the centuries. Humankind has always sought clues to our meaning and purpose through the wonders of the natural world because of an intrinsic sense of the energies that inhabit and weave together all of life. The ancients regarded the patterns of the stars not only as Divine omens, but as energetic templates for decoding the patterns of light carried in our Divine souls and in the desires, purposes and potentials expressed through our human personalities. Discerning that the Divine-Human mysteries are encoded in the natural world and in all of Creation through number, quality and patterning, the wise men of the past studied the constellations of stars and other heavenly bodies, and all of nature's forms and ways, as a serious spiritual science. It was only when the medieval Christian church declared the study of the stars and Earth rites to be heretical in order to establish absolute authority and power for the church, that these were relegated to "occult," "pagan" and even "demonic" sciences.

Keynote phrase: This is a short by-line I have added to capture the essence of the Angel's function.

Overlighting Archangel: This is the Archangel that governs the Sephira which the Angel resides within on the Tree of Life, and whose qualities overlight or influence the functions of the eight Angels in that Sephira and the Angelic order (choir) that the Angels belong to. There are eight Angels in each of the Nine (out of Ten) Sephirot on the Tree (8x9=72). Because so many people working with Angels in our modern world seem to be working with the Archangel energies, it is perhaps interesting to note that throughout the world's Angelic traditions and the ancient wisdoms, Archangels' were seen as the guardians of lands, nations and societal groups; whereas the Angels are said to be attendant to individuals because their vibrations are nearer to life forms. However, until this tradition was revealed in the 1980's-90's by the work of Kabaleb through his own and Haziel's books, only a few of the Angels' individual names have been commonly known to modern angelology.

The Angel's sign, planet and 5-day period of "Incarnation" influence: The Angel's astrological correspondences relate to its five consecutive days of influence once a year on the Incarnation, or physical, plane, which also corresponds to 5 degrees of the Zodiac (72x5=360) – taking into consideration the adjustments made for a 365-day year (see Appendix I). If you are interested in astrology, this can help to shed additional light on the Angel's qualities. (Neptune and Uranus were added later when they were discovered.) Although the Angels in their Incarnation influence (physicality, will and life purpose) are not the focus of the *Book of Days*, I added the dates of each Angel's Incarnation influence (the date spread next to the sign/planet) for ease in discovering your Incarnation Angel – which would be the one supporting the five-day span that corresponds to the five-days around your birth. For example, if your birthday is March 18, your Incarnation Angel would be #72 MUMIAH, which governs March 16-20. However, because of the yearly fluctuation of degrees correspondent to days, if your birthday is the first or last day or the Angel's date-span of support, then it is suggested to pay attention to the Angel closest to yours, being the previous or next, whichever applies – and notice which is more resonant. (See also Appendix I for a complete list of the 72 Angels with their corresponding 5-day span of Incarnation influence, as well as the 20-minute period during the 24-hour day when they support our intellect.)

"I AM THAT WHICH...:" Here the Angel introduces itself as a particularized aspect ("that which") of the One "I AM" which is its purpose to amplify in our human lives – thus helping us to fulfill the unique "I Am That Which" that each of us are as a particular constellation and expression of Divine-Human qualities.

The Angel's message: As detailed above, all 72 Angels cycle for at least one day five times a year, effectively taking us through the seasons of the year and of our lives. Since everything and everyone exists in the context of relationship, the first cycle of 72 messages starting March 21 starts with the new birth of the natural world which also symbolizes the soul's cosmic birth and relationship to the Divine. From there we move into the four subsequent cycles – our relationship with self, our work and purposes, others in our close circles, and then to our communities and the world at large.

Thus, all five cycles comprise a journey in one year through all the literal and symbolic themes and seasons of our lives.

You will likely notice that the Angels have different tones in their "speech" at different times – some are lighter, some more serious, some "teacherly" and others passionate. Also, sometimes an they speak as "I" and sometimes as "we." I continue to sense that in their roles as differentiated expressions of the Divine Oneness, "I" and "we" are interchangeable for them. The messages of course come through my own within and are mingled with the vocabularies and meanings which I am able to discern – and the more I bring myself into the present with love, the more and better I am able to hear. The light-thread that is woven through all the different messages is about the power of love to reveal and expand the truth of who we are and what we are here to be and do for ourselves, each other and the Divine Itself.

The "Amen" at the end of each Wisdom. I realized I had been hearing "Amen" at the end of each Wisdom from the beginning of the *Book of Days* and had not been fully conscious of it until working on the third volume! "Amen" is a word of power in Hebrew, a kind of cosmic "abracadabra" to activate the Divine in human life. In researching the word's origins, there were the usual Hebrew and Christian uses of Amen as "so be it" at the end of prayers, as well as other correspondences: Amen encompasses the Hebrew letters "aleph-mem-nun" (confirmed, reliable, have faith, believe), which also correspond to the word "emuna" (faith) and "emet" (truth). There are also associations with the Egyptian god Amun (also Amen, the creator of all things, king of the gods) and the Hindu Sanskrit word Aum (or Om, the Absolute, Omnipresent, Manifest and Unmanifest). In suddenly becoming fully aware of the "Amen" that was naturally emerging at the end of each wisdom, I realized that the intent of the Angelic Energy was that the words would not only inspire but also *transmit* the energies of their meaning unto those "who have the heart to hear." In the cacophony of life and its demands, we may have the heart to hear in one moment and not in another – so the word Amen is a word to call us back to our hearts from wherever else we are. And so here, as "Amen...," the three dots are meant to extend a loving and compassionate space to do that.

Remember, again, that the Daily Wisdoms are given as messages from the 72 Angels when they are in their "heart dominion," to amplify qualities of Divine Love to support our cultivation of self-love and love of others, as well the other resources of the heart which are compassion, understanding, forgiveness, intuition, soul-truth and wisdom. As the Angel JELIEL conveys in Volume 1,

> *The Love we bring is a Love composed of as many different qualities, forms, faces and expressions as there are people...a Love that contains all purposes and possibilities...a Love that will be your anchor against time's fickle winds of change and the sometimes stormy seas of life. A Love-light of Truth by which you may see finally that however long or far you seek, what you are looking for is always right here in your heart of hearts, prompting you to ask, beckoning you to receive, inviting you to shine forth more and more of who you truly are. And to know once and for all that, truly, you are not alone – for there is always someone at home...within.*

And so now, may you continue your daily heart-journey with the 72 Angels, the joy of the season's inward bounty and the nurturing of new seeds in your heart, mind, body and soul!

January 9 – 16

Angels 1 – 8

Sephira 1

KETHER ~ Crown/Will

Overlighting Archangel

METATRON ~ "Angel of the Presence"
Enlightenment, the connection of Light between
God's energy and human spiritual energy
(Related to the prophet Enoch & Akashic Records)

---

1 VEHUIAH
2 JELIEL
3 SITAEL
4 ELEMIAH
5 MAHASIAH
6 LELAHEL
7 ACHAIAH
8 CAHETEL

3/21 * 6/3 * 8/17 * 10/30 * **1/9**

1 VEHUIAH

(vay-HOO-ee-YAH)

Will and New Beginnings (G)

'One who begins again and again'

Archangel ~ METATRON

Aries / Uranus (3/21-25)

I AM THAT WHICH...

provides the light-energy and impetus to initiate innovation, inventions, inroads and new courses of action to benefit group functioning and community dynamics. In the 'data bank' of light within and around you are the wisdoms and creations forged by those who came before and paved the way, so that where and how you are going forward now individually and together might become possible. Honor and draw from those wisdoms for the birthing of new ideas, forms and pathways. If you start or acquire a new enterprise, probe those with more experience for what they have learned – even if you are highly skilled. Regard each other without assumption or presumption, knowing that the group dynamic is composed of individual energies and ways of being and doing that reflect unique purposes and styles. Use your will rightly so that the wills of others are respected and even inspired, whatever position you may hold in the hierarchy of the group. If you are a leader, know that it is up to you to set an inclusive and affirming tone for the collaborative experience.

Know especially that it is the uniqueness of each of you as individuals that yields your gifts and contributions to the whole. Although there will need to be group agreements in order to 'get things done,' let your agreements not be from the pressure to conform. Rather, approach each other with your hearts and minds toward mutual inclusivity and appreciation of your diverse individualities. Learn from each other, that you may broaden and deepen your own capacities. Allow the magic of the new to gestate among you – and especially to bring forth creations together that none would have brought forth on your own.

Thus, dear innovative thinkers and co-creators, I offer you my 'first light' as VEHUIAH that you might see the infinite possibilities of new becomings 'where two or more are gathered.' Let the dawning of new light be warm and gentle among you, encouraging the seeding of ideas in a co-creative atmosphere where each contribution is a gift that helps the whole to increase information, knowledge and wisdom as you collaborate on your goal. Even be willing to forego 'how it was always done' in order to create new ways and means that will better serve the needs of your community and world as it is now. Let the past not imprison the present, but be a teacher and inspirer of the future.

And in all your beginnings, dear ones, let the combined resources of your hearts – love, compassion, intuition, wisdom and understanding – be the guiding light for the implementation of your intentions and goals that they may be beneficial and life-affirming for all. Amen...

3/22 * 6/4 * 8/18 + 19am * 10/31 * **1/10**

2 JELIEL

(YAY-lee-EL)

Love and Wisdom (G)

'One who uses love to make wisdom'

Archangel ~ METATRON

Aries / Saturn (3/26-30)

I AM THAT WHICH...

helps to reinvigorate the fire of love within you so that you might do your part to magnify the power of groups and gatherings for loving and beneficent action in the world. Each of you holds a piece of the bigger-picture puzzle of life. Each of you has gifts and talents that only you have. And the more love you have – of self, of life and each other, the more enthusiasm you will have for not only your own dreams and purposes, but also for being an inspiration and help to others. It is in loving yourself that you may come to know who you are, for it is love's 'job' on Earth to expand the truth of you. And it is the love and truth of you that the world needs for its own greaterness – no matter how much the world may test and try you to make you strong enough to be yourself.

If you want to be wise, you must especially have love for your own being – and love for the mysteries of your soul, even though it may take your whole life and beyond to discover them. For only love sees more than meets the eye in yourself and others. Only love has compassion for what cannot seem to be understood or forgiven. Only love knows hurt and hate is just love longing to be acknowledged. Only love puts all the lost pieces back together in a new way when everything has fallen apart. Only love can truly transform you, the others and your world into the greater truth of who you can be together.

And so, know that every hole in the world is started by a hole in the heart of a single hurting one – one who cannot bear the pain of unbelonging or disappointment, the kindness that does not come, the dream that remains elusive, the society that seems to shut him out again and again. Such a one has forgotten what his soul meant to do with his humanness and how much the world truly needs him for what only he can give. Such a one has forgotten that she is so loved by the Divine Itself that the Divine dwells within her, waiting to be recognized, waiting to be loved back.

And so dear one and ones, my work within you as the JELIEL love-light of the Divine is to love you as the inner beloved that has always been within you, as you, and thus may never be parted from you. Your fragile world, and even more fragile Earth, needs the authentic and brave heart of you, that you may bring your love, compassion and wisdom to everything that is multiplied and magnified in your gatherings with others. So love yourself, and help others to do the same by loving them to show them how it is done. Love is the key and the door, the way in and the way out, the why and wherefore, the opportunity and wonder of being fully alive in your togetherness and co-creations. With love as the glue, go forth with your sisters and brothers and put your hearts and your world back together. Amen...

3/23 * 6/5 * 8/19pm + 20 * 11/1 * **1/11**

3 SITAEL

(SIT-ah-EL)

Construction of Worlds (G)

'One who loves creations into being'

Archangel ~ METATRON

Aries / Jupiter (3/31-4/4)

I AM THAT WHICH...

helps you to come together with others to create constructs and structures in your world that reflect the values and meanings you hold dear in your individual and collective hearts. As the Divine Architect's worlds and works are built with infinite forms of matter for the sake of the essence and meaning that animate them, let this be a template for your own worldly constructions. Put your heart and soul into whatever you create in the physical world, and your creations will have the vitality and energy to send endless ripples of enlivening and inspiration across your world unto others and their creations.

It is the delight of your humanity to give structure to your personal and communal worlds. How glorious to see tangible manifestations of the greatness and diversity of human feeling and thought fulfilled in renderings of stone, wood, metals and all the materials of Earth and humankind. Only here upon this privilege of Earth can you experience the power and glory of employing both the tangible and intangible aspects of your totality to form and functionalize matter – and especially as physical and vibrational 'holding patterns' for what has meaning, value and essential mattering to the human spirit.

You refer to those who work with their hands as craftsmen – but it is any work done with heart that creates the most eternally resonant value. As the vagaries of time bring a patina of age and wear to handmade forms, the creation energies of love with which they were made does not diminish. This is evident especially in your inspired works of art, music and literature which outlive time itself. But even in your edifices, organizations, corporations and governments, their meanings, values and impact will always outlast their material configurations.

Thus I SITAEL say – create lovingly and truly, and when forms fall or fade away, gather up any noble intentions which gave them life, and re-build. Allow newly-emerging truths to strengthen and ennoble new constructions. And while many of your technologies mimic the functions of mind, your inventions and societies will benefit greatly to also include more of the feeling and value-based designs held within your visionary hearts. Bring these value-based templates also to your organizations, corporations and governments that they might reflect the life-affirming values you hold most dear. Despite the 'rush to market' of 'consumerism,' let your outer creations be built first in the inner humus of heart and soul – letting the seeds of ideas gestate and be nurtured within you. For if you create something true in the integrity of your small circle, it will be empowered to find the life that is its potential in the greater world. Trust in your co-creativity with love, and it will bring your co-creations into life-affirming and beneficent being in their true time. So it shall be. Amen...

3/24 * 6/6 * 8/21 * 11/2 * **1/12**

4 ELEMIAH

(eh-LEM-ee-YAH)

Divine Power (G)

'One who implants the tree of life within'

Archangel ~ METATRON

Aries / Mars (4/5-9)

I AM THAT WHICH...

helps to cultivate the right use of power in your societal, business and government structures and to help use power struggles as opportunities to realign with higher principles and values that empower all concerned in true and complementary ways. The shortsightedness in all 'special interests' and battles of power is blindness to the fact that you are all part of one great whole, and that ultimately the whole will weaken if any are continually disenfranchised. The thriving of the group is dependent upon the thriving of all individuals within it. And when the group thrives, it has the power, in turn, to continue to support its members. It is when the group uses the resources of individuals to support only a few that the group becomes weakened, which further erodes the well-being of all. Power that does not feed people, but rather feeds off of them is a force that ultimately brings starvation to all, even the self-interested who mistakenly think their gain will inoculate them from consequence. For power used in this way is only a temporal power of position or barter, which is always vulnerable to time and the power of others.

The only power on Earth which is unlimited is the power of love. I offer you to know, as the ELEMIAH light-power which I am, that Love is the power that expands and regenerates the authenticity, the 'I Am,' of each and all beingness. It is this same power that continues the essence of life by regenerating new forms from the seeds of those that have fallen away. What seeds will you leave behind to nourish those who come after you? Seeds of love or fear? Seeds of wholeness or fragmentation? It is yours to choose, but that said, love will use all choices as a compost to enrich the soil of life from which love will continue to spring forth in the hearts, dreams and creations of all new life.

We desire you also to deeply understand that the power of the human aspects of your Divine-Human beingness is naturally and beautifully linked with the power of the Earth. The resiliency and renewal that is inherent in the humus of your humanity is exampled and supported by the power of the natural world to regenerate itself season after season – just as the new cells of your own body regenerate you, and newborn beings regenerate humankind. Align with the intelligent powers of nature to quicken the natural intelligence of your being for renewal and thriving. Let the natural world show you how to be here with yourselves and each other – how to give and receive the gifts of shelter and interdependence that living things and creatures can offer to each other, how to rely on your unique diversities to strengthen the whole, how to withstand and flow with the winds of change, how to use the seeds of a season's end to prepare for the next season's new beginning. For indeed, the natural world is given not only as an ally to sustain you, but as a mirror for your own hidden powers that you might awaken unto your greatness. Amen...

3/25 * 6/7 * 8/22 * 11/3 * **1/13**

5 MAHASIAH

(ma-HA-see-YAH)

Rectification (G)

'One who returns to what is true for love's sake'

Archangel ~ METATRON

Aries / Sun (4/10-14)

I AM THAT WHICH...

helps to correct the misguided functioning of a group, community, organization or government by helping you and the other individuals involved to bring your own values and sensibilities of what is true, right and loving to the group. All group agreements and creations are born of collective individuals, but the group itself is a construct – and you cannot heal the construct without healing those who constructed it. You may ask, 'what can one person do?' Corporations and governments are often brought down by the pride, greed and delusions of one person – who may be sanctioned by those around him through bartered cooperation, denial, fear or blind obedience. And while you certainly have many examples in your histories of what one person can do to cause the eradication of thousands and millions of people, there are many more who have uplifted and changed all future history for the better by implanting higher values into the hearts and minds of generations.

The breakdown of your societal, business and government constructs occurs when members protect their self-interests at the exclusion or expense of others. It is often difficult for even the best leadership to break through the entanglements and entitlements of collective and conflicting self-interests. Thus it is more imperative for the 'common man,' who may seem to be rendered powerless by the 'power-mongers,' to self-empower and become more aware and responsive. You – one person – can bring your own higher values to the 'bottom lines' and 'operating protocols' of your personal ways of living and working – and from there to your collaborations and constructs with others.

My rectifying light as MAHASIAH is given for you to see the connections between your own personal values and ways of being and how these are reflected in all your group constructs, communities, governments and world. Your own wholeness is absolutely vital to the healing and wholeness of all. Imagine if wholeness were the bottom line in your family and friendship groups. Imagine if personal and collective development and well-being was part of the agenda in every community. Imagine if every person on Earth undertook to create a meaningful, purposeful life – each in ways that are life-affirming and most passionately relevant to your being. Imagine living in a society in which 'every man for himself' gave way to the support of 'everyman' by your communities to help all of you achieve your dreams and goals. Perhaps you would be too busy becoming personally and collectively fulfilled to argue over ideologies and national borders!

Dear ones, the world and all the heavens feel the ripples of your every act, for nothing you do is a secret to the all-knowing of love. Everything can be used for love, if you are willing, and there is nothing you have ever done that cannot be turned into love, for the sake of you and all and the Divine Heart that cradles you from within. Amen...

3/26 * 6/8 * 8/23 * 11/4 * **1/14**

6 LELAHEL

(LAY-la-HEL)

Light of Understanding (G)

'One who transforms knowledge'

Archangel ~ METATRON

Aries / Venus (4/15-20)

I AM THAT WHICH...

helps you to pause your reactions to actions and events in your communities and the world in order to see them in a different light – which can reveal underlying factors, original causes, 'domino effects' and the parts everyone has played in everything that happens. Many things that occur in your world are a result of immediate reactions and judgments, the effects of which are often 'stockpiled' and reactivated continually, even for generations. What you see, what you are told and hear, is usually just what 'breaks the surface' – like the island that is the topmost peak of a whole mountain hidden beneath the waters. To understand issues and conflicts in groups, organizations, cultures and governments, you must understand not only the present context and the desires of the individuals involved, but the historical setting and what has been building in the collective psyche that is coming to the surface to be released and even possibly healed. And if all that is too much to consider, then just pause for a breath before or after your reaction to consider that there is likely more involved that is beyond your current access or understanding.

The 'true truths' of what goes on in the 'back rooms' of the earthly 'powers that be' are hidden from public view. The claims of 'transparency' yield only what those powers want you to know based on an agenda that is likely very different from yours.

Creativity in your world serves many masters! Some use it to shrink and isolate possibility for the benefit of the few, and some use it to expand possibility for everyone. No matter how powerless the seemingly powerful can make you feel, you too have powers – and they are far greater than barter and position, despite the access these seem to purchase for those who have them.

Dear heart, my light as LELAHEL lovingly illuminates that your true powers are innate to you. These are the powers of your heart, foremost of which is love, and all the other powers which love gives you access to – compassion, understanding, forgiveness, insight, intuition and wisdom. Look at what is happening in your world through the eyes of love and you will understand the 'truer truths' that no 'top secret' access could give you. Because even those who hold the clandestine secrets of the world do not themselves know the whole truth. If they did, they wouldn't be trying to hide or sequester it for the benefit of the few.

You can only understand as much as you are willing to love*. In love's light you can see that all are connected, and everyone – consciously or unconsciously, willfully or for lack of will, ancestrally or personally – contributes to every act of harm or help in your world. Your personal power of understanding is to open heart and mind and be willing to see what has not been seen, hear what has not been said and feel what is yet still a longing just beneath the surface of every heart and happening. Amen...*

3/27 * 6/9 * 8/24 * 11/5 * **1/15**

7 ACHAIAH

(a-KA-hee-YAH)

Patience (G)

'One who brings the stillness'

Archangel ~ METATRON

Taurus / Mercury (4/21-25)

I AM THAT WHICH...

helps to exercise patience and the willingness to allow information and events to unfold and be considered with thoughtfulness and wisdom. In your human urges to know, act and possess, there is often impatience. The problem with impatience is that it takes you out of the natural flow of evolving information that is already on its way to you and all involved. With patience you can sense that there is 'more to the story.' By hanging back a bit, you give it room to be revealed and find its way to you without force or contrivance. Patience can seem weak or passive to those who think that making an aggressive show of willfulness, bravado or force is a strength – but only the truly strong and wise know how to utilize patience to increase the possibility for best outcomes.

Patience, and the gestation it allows, is so necessary to your innate power to bring about change and renewal that there is even a whole season that provides you the time to practice it! In the natural world, the winter days between fall and spring render outer forms seemingly dormant, allowing the seeds of things-to-come to gestate in the soil of time. Likewise, the pause you take between an event and your response provides time for those involved to become aware of and reveal their true feelings, motives or underlying agendas, and for your own wisdom to inform and form your ultimate response. In both your personal and public life, seasons of seeming dormancy allow you and others time for rumination, reevaluation and the seeds of new ideas, endeavors and ways to begin to take root.

Group patience must be supported by the wisdom of its members. Often it is the emotional reactivity and hastiness of just one person that can turn a single word into an argument, one incident into a wave of hysteria, a crowd into an out of control 'mob' – or a misguided piece of military intelligence into a full-scale war.

Thus, dear humanly impatient ones, I invite you to draw on my ACHAIAH light to trust the flow and learn how to wait. And may you also use the time of waiting to transform impatience into compassion and wisdom in order to gain a deeper understanding of a person or circumstance that involves more than what you want for yourself. Wait for a true time to ripen. Use my eternal light to raise your inner gaze to the bigger picture of the effects your actions will have when they are experienced by the other, or multiplied by the many. Be one of the heart-minded ones who use right timing to strengthen friendship, community or any group or organization you are part of. Let periods of stillness remind you that the eternal will give you all the time you or the other needs, and more. Trust the flow, trust love and truth, trust yourself – and be the HEART you want to see in the world. Amen...

3/28 * 6/10 * 8/25 * 11/6 * **1/16**

8 CAHETEL

(KA-heh-TEL)

Divine Blessings (G)

'One who conducts the flow of plenty'

Archangel ~ METATRON

Taurus / Moon (4/26-30)

I AM THAT WHICH...

helps you to realize the blessings of the Earth and all beings which contribute to the care and sustenance of all, and to do your part as an individual seed within humankind to help protect, sustain and increase your mutual bounty. The greatest blessings you have been given for your journey on this Earth are each other. This includes all the different species of living beings, and the Earth itself as the physical sustainer of all. In addition, if you care for and receive the blessings of the Earth in gratitude and cooperation, you come to know that it provides not only your physical sustenance, but the spiritual 'life codes' that reveal the mysteries of life and creation and how much more you are and can be than your physical selves would seem to allow. Those who have lived close to the Earth are wise in this, and thus when nature's beings have been continually exploited to proliferate 'progress' and material profit, you cut yourselves off from the wisdom and protection of the Earth.

Your world is full of plenty, but the yield of plenty involves balance and attunement with the nature of things and beings. Because all living beings are sourced from the energies of Divine creation, all life is inherently regenerative, capable of bringing forth more life from itself. However, you can directly affect quantity and quality of plenty by your caring attention, respect and love. Just ask any gardener! The very things your small garden needs are also what the Earth and all beings need: healthy nutrient-rich soil, clean water and air, the warmth and light of the sun, conducive temperatures, a balance between creative and destructive forces – and especially – co-creative stewards that understand, respect and work within the rhythms of the seasons and the natural forces that come together to bring ripening and abundance. As your key to ensuring and increasing abundance is to work dynamically ***with*** *the Earth's natural resources and their natural flow – not in spite of them – so is it key to embrace all beings as integral to the richness of your humanity and the vitality of all species with whom you co-habit the Earth.*

In the natural world, the diverse flora and fauna of the Earth have an innate natural intelligence and interdepend-dence that ensures their continuation. If you continually inject elements that disturb these, chaos in the natural order of mutual life support systems will occur. Even if this seems to increase yield for a time – the depletion of quality in favor of quantity will ultimately corrupt the 'humus' and health of the human body and being, and thus eventually all humankind and living species. But this doesn't have to be if you tap some of your own greatest inner resources – awareness and your birthright to choose and change.

At the root of partaking more fully in your natural resources at every level of life, individually and collectively, are three things that could hugely impact your world for the better: (1) to ease the desire for immediate gratification, and the continual need for more and more, by trusting the plentiful nature and timing of life and entering into its wondrous flow without impeding or forcing it (2) to truly and deeply realize the ***fact*** *that everything and everyone on your planet – including your planetary and galactic atmospheres, fields and bodies – are all interconnected and impactful upon each other, and (3) to understand and embrace the* ***fact*** *that diversity is key to your survival because each thing and being contributes something the others don't have, thus enriching each and adding to the energy, vitality and enrichment of the whole.*

The birth of otherness from the One, and a third from two, are the great cosmic blessings of creation and regeneration that continually expand life. How do you participate in and multiply these Divine blessings? By being a blessing to each other – through mutual companionship, kindness, giving and receiving. By being each other's soft landings, helping hands and comforting shoulders. By extending leeway, latitude and non-judgment. Through seeing more than meets the eye by looking with your heart. By seeing your diversities as the contrast that inspires you to define and fine-tune your own uniqueness. By seeing your sameness of heart and the spirit of love and life that dwells within each of you and is expressed outwardly so uniquely. By realizing that the animals, trees and other flora are your friends, teachers and co-creators, and that all things of the Earth are alive and sentient beings, affected by everything you think, feel and do.

And so, dear innately resilient and bountiful one, may you partake of my blessing light as CAHETEL to see that you and all beings are the natural resources of the Earth itself – and that the Earth relies on you as much as you rely on it. Thus, may you go forth and multiply your individual life-affirming choices to help create and sustain a greater Earth and a more whole and cooperative world with your fellow beings and the Earth itself. Amen...

January 17 – 24

Angels 9 – 16

Sephira 2

CHOKMAH ~ Wisdom

Overlighting Archangel

RAZIEL ~ 'Secrets of God'
Spiritual guidance, keeper of wisdom
and revealer of the mysteries

---

9 HAZIEL
10 ALADIAH
11 LAUVIAH
12 HAHAIAH
13 YEZALEL
14 MEBAHEL
15 HARIEL
16 HAKAMIAH

3/29 * 6/11 * 8/26 * 11/7 * **1/17**

9 HAZIEL

(HA-zee-EL)

Divine Mercy and Forgiveness (S)

'One who sees with the light of love'

Archangel ~ RAZIEL

Taurus / Uranus (5/1-5)

I AM THAT WHICH...

helps you to be merciful and forgiving to yourself and others through the awareness that all of humanity are as leaves on one great Tree of Life, and that the Tree is good and beneficent by virtue of its Divinely-endowed existence. Thus, to withhold anything from anyone that is in your power to give, or not yours to withhold, is to withhold from yourself – and likewise, to withhold from yourself what is freely yours is to withhold it from all. Just as every act of transgression is felt by all, every act of mercy and forgiveness restores the sovereignty of love which is also felt by all.

In a perceived wrongdoing by any person or group, it is very common with the passing of time, and even generations, to lose sight of when the 'worm first burrowed into the apple.' One act begets another and that begets another, and so on and on – because in the polarities of physical life, for every action there is a reaction, as you say. The cure for this is not more blame, judgment, punishment, or 'an eye for an eye' vengeance, because these only perpetuate more of the same. The cure is to interrupt the cycles of hurt with love, mercy and compassion. Every time you extend compassion to others, you awaken their own capacities for compassion. As compassion is seeded in your relatings, the paradigm of loving-kindness takes root which enables you to begin to heal the transgressions and tragedies which occur among you.

Dear heart, I invite you to use my merciful HAZIEL light to see that when you give and receive mercy and forgiveness, you are initiated into the mysteries of the Divine Heart beyond time, place and physical form. Here, in this field of infinite love you may come to know that you are intrinsically good and that mercy and forgiveness among you are just ways to bring the soul-memory of that into the awareness of your humanity. For in the Divine Heart, there is nothing to forgive. Each of your souls inhabit human form in order to express, experience and learn with and through each other and to give the Divine an experience of physical life as only you can live it.

Must you forgive your own children for being born? Do you not fold into your parenting the knowing that you will love your children no matter what, simply because they are your children? This is the safety of love that all children need – and which you as a child of the Divine are enfolded within. Nothing you can ever do will either deserve or divest you of this infinite mercy. For you are not born in sin, but in love... even as love itself. Amen...

3/30 * 6/12 + 13am * 8/27 * 11/8 * **1/18**

10 ALADIAH

(a-LA-dee-YAH)

Divine Grace (G)

'One who endows you with the yes of life'

Archangel ~ RAZIEL

Taurus / Saturn (5/6-10)

I AM THAT WHICH...

brings the fluidity and softness of love to temper the rigidity of rules, dogma, tradition or status quo in order to allow time and space for learning and growth through the seasons and cycles of your humanity. It is grace that brings the Divine into all things human through love and compassion – by infusing meaning into matter, spirit into ritual and practice, quality into quantity, heart into speech and action, and the how and why into every what. And it is grace that has the power to transform every difficult happening in your world into an opportunity for healing and transcendence. Through grace you call forth humanity from inhumane actions, love from expressions of hate, forgiveness from hurt, mercy from judgment, change from stagnation, and freedom even amidst the tyrannies of oppression. From your most personal to public trials and travesties, grace is the bringer of second chances and new beginnings after every seeming failure and finality.

Through your own hearts the Divine Heart is disseminated between and among you. You have the power invested in you by Divine Grace to be each other's miracles of possibility and illumination of meaning and purpose. For grace – born of the Divine Heart within yours – is not something you do, but something you receive and give to each other from within which has no merit or measure, no judgment or expectation, no investment in return or reward.

Thus dear one, I invite you to partake of my ALADIAH grace-light to illuminate what part of the Divine you bring to the world through your unique gifts and willingness of heart. If you wonder what one person can do to change the world, remember the Divine within you and each, and look to the impossible that Divine Love has again and again manifested unto many through one willing and compassionate human heart. In doing what cannot be done so that people and dreams can become possible, Divine Grace is truly your 'saving' grace. And the more you receive, the more you have to give, and the more you give, the more there is. And the more there is, the more healing comes to the world, near and far, far and wide. All starting with you. So open your heart, and let it be so. Amen...

3/31 * 6/13pm + 14 * 8/28 * 11/9 * **1/19**

11 LAUVIAH

(LO-vee-YAH)

Victory (G)

'One who turns every moment into a win'

Archangel ~ RAZIEL

Taurus / Jupiter (5/11-15)

I AM THAT WHICH...

inspires you to support the outcome you desire rather than fight the one you don't – and to know that true victory, which belongs to the one who wins the battle that cannot be fought, is possible only if everyone wins. True victory is not an event, but a way. The true victor does not fight against a negative situation, but takes action in support of a positive one. When you fight against a thing, you may win numerous battles, but you will lose the greater war as you become consumed with and contaminated by the fight itself. This holds true not only in worldly battles for righteous causes, but also for the battles of daily existence, relationships and personal inner conflict between opposing desires. Thus, invite your 'opposition' to the higher ground of the heart to discover what it is that each part or party wants and how all may win what they need or desire.

It takes great humility to win a slow victory. You may carry a sense of the bigger picture, but you must put in the time and effort to fill in all the pieces. There may not be a way to get there as the crow flies, so you may have to pass through many valleys and climb one mountain after another. The days may be dark and the nights long, and you may have to wait for a seeming eternity for a season of attitudes and old conditionings to change. You may feel lost at times and forget what it is that you were ever seeking. But know this: like the Divine Itself, you are always seeking your Self –

whatever other name you may call it. So follow the call within and you will see the dark in a different light. Love the bigger picture and it will attract the true pieces that only your heart knows what to do with. Revel in the winding road and the valleys and the mountains for they will show you vistas in your soul and in the hearts and souls of others that you didn't know were there. Love the thing you seek, and it is you who will be found, within yourself and in the other.

Dear brave one, I show you with my LAUVIAH light that true victory is won not only for one, but for each and all – and the possibility for that victory lives in your heart and in the sameness between your heart and another. No matter what the seeming, you cannot win through stubbornness, pride, greed, fear, judgment, hate or revenge – lest what is won is the ashes of all you lost to win it. And also know that in any kind of battle, there may come a moment when surrender is called for, so that we, your Angelic allies, may shine forth the Divine Brilliance by which all things might be seen and resolved in a greater light – the light that can only be harnessed from the higher ground of your Divine-Human heart. Amen...

4/1 * 6/15 * 8/29 * 11/10 * **1/20**

12 HAHAIAH

(ha-HA-ee-YAH)

Refuge, Shelter (G)

'One who is a beacon of shelter within'

Archangel ~ RAZIEL

Taurus / Mars (5/16-20)

I AM THAT WHICH...

helps you to bring your personal sense of refuge and shelter to the greater world by respecting the Earth as your sacred communal home and community as a place to extend the support of heart and shoulder to each other. Among the graces you have within you to offer others – whether loved ones, colleagues or seeming strangers – are the embrace and 'envelopment' of empathy and caring – even if for only a moment. Think about what and who makes you feel sheltered in your own life. Home, a space and place to come back to, is an obvious first – but the true shelter in any home is composed of the people within it, and feeling emotionally 'safe' with them. Whether these are people you are physically living with, or a network of family and friends near and far, true shelter happens among those who guard each other's hopes and dreams, who want the best for each other, who see potential and nurture it, who let you leave off striving for a bit and accept the moments and days when it's just too hard or tiring to do one's best – and when the soft landing of a heart or a strong shoulder is what is needed most.

When you have this close support in your life, it is easier to take it out into the world. But you can also find and create a sense of interconnection and refuge in the world at large when you really begin to see that you are all one great interconnected family of humankind on the earthly tree of life – and that the root system which sustains you all is the intertwining inner and outer realms of the Divine, the Human and the natural world. Indeed, the natural world is not only your physical sustainer, but a living example and teacher of how to be shelter and refuge for each other. How to stand together to withstand the storms of life, and yet not so close that you stifle each other's growth. How species totally different from each other live in close proximity and offer mutual gifts of nurturing, nourishment and support that are unique to each.

The need for refuge exists in every species and goes way beyond the physical – for it is not only primal, but primeval. Home is both an instinct and a soul-urge. There are those who don't have homes in the usual sense of the word. And yet, the urge for refuge is so great that they find a way to create a sense of proprietary space – a strip of sidewalk or desert, a cardboard box, a tent, a car, a friendship, a 'social network' – any kind of touchstone in a community within which they feel most 'at home,' even when homeless.

I offer you my HAHAIAH light of refuge so that you might come to feel the home of Heaven as any place on Earth where you can bring your heart to another in mutual recognition and kindness. You carry your true home within you, in your heart of hearts. So wherever you go, wherever you are, 'come home to your heart' dear one and be embraced by the refuge of love. Amen...

4/2 * 6/16 * 8/30 * 11/11 * **1/21**

13 YEZALEL

(YAY-za-LEL)

Fidelity, Loyalty and Allegiance (G)

'One who keeps faith with the inner Divine'

Archangel ~ RAZIEL

Gemini / Sun (5/21-25)

I AM THAT WHICH...

helps to cultivate trust, affinity, loyalty and a foundational environment for productivity by drawing those of like mind and heart together for a shared vision that aspires to higher principles and a greater good. It is the disparity between personal values and worldly loyalties that causes much of the individual and collective heartache in the world. Thus, it is important to realize that any allegiance which undermines the well-being of yourself or your loved ones, colleagues or community is a loyalty that betrays the soul of the world and the soul, or meaning, in all you do. You can no more serve two masters than 22. Serve the master of true-selfness within and let your worldly loyalties line up accordingly. Doing so, in tandem with others doing the same in their own ways, creates a collective that supports you as individuals – which then comes full circle to support and strengthen the collective. 'To thine own self be true' so that you may bring trueness and self-sovereigty to the world, rather than a conflicted and fractured self. In collective loyalty to what is noble and true, you will be unbreakable like a 'bundle of sticks.'

Ultimately, anything or anyone that you betray becomes a betrayal and underminer of yourself. Thus, you cannot betray even yourself in order to be loyal to the world and have the world remain loyal to you, because self-betrayal betrays the integrity of the world. Just as you cannot be disloyal to the Earth which is your natural ally, and expect her to remain loyal to you. Not because the Earth will purposefully act against you, but because lack of fidelity to that which sustains you will weaken it to the point where it becomes unable to do so.

For example, pollute the clean air you are given to breathe, and ultimately the air will become unbreathable. Corrupt the integrity of the soil and the waters that provide you with food and drink, and their bounties will become unpalatable. Those who live and work closely with the Earth know that she is a living and sentient being, your great Mother-provider, given to not only sustain you physically – but to teach you about the natural passages of life, resiliency of the essence which lives on, and especially the importance of diversity in the dynamics of interdependence which enable greater thriving for all.

Thus do I offer you my YEZALEL light that you may bring individually and together the values of your heart to all beings and to the soil and soul of the Earth and her creations. Seed your relatings and collaborations with the care and wisdom of your heart, so that all you create may be resilient and supportive of you and all the parts of the whole. Come together with an allegiance to what is noble and life-affirming, that your faithfulness will enable all of life to keep faith with you. Amen...

4/3 * 6/17 * 8/31 * 11/12 * **1/22**

14 MEBAHEL

(MAY-ba-HEL)

Truth, Liberty and Justice (G)

'One who is freed by Truth to set Truth itself free'

Archangel ~ RAZIEL

Gemini / Venus (5/26-31)

I AM THAT WHICH...

brings the light of understanding that it takes every truth of every being in all of creation, seen and unseen, to compose and illuminate the many hues and expressions of the whole Truth, and thus, each person's experience of Truth is vital to the wholeness of humankind. Each of you are so loved that you are met by the Divine 'I Am' that is Truth itself on any road, path or pathlessness, in any creed, culture, vocabulary or expression that most speaks to and evokes your heart. The 'whole Truth' represents the absolute I Am of the Divine that is revealed and infinitely expanded through Love. Thus, particular aspects of Divine Truth are 'echoed' in and expressed by each created being as a relative truth of that all-encompassing absolute Truth.

In other words, you each represent and express a piece of the whole Truth – one that is most relevant to you and the purposes and potentials of your soul within your human incarnation in this life. The 'problems' of divisiveness begin when a particular relative truth spawns group agreements and ideologies that promote it as an 'only truth.' And then inclusionary and exclusionary 'rules' of belief and behavior turn that 'only truth' into a tool for dissent, persecution, and worse. Every time this manipulation and contrivance of Truth occurs, the very nature of Truth is negated and its liberating powers are diminished – and so are yours.

No one experience, belief, creed or dogma can contain all of Truth. Because of Love, the manifestations of Truth in creation are relevant, fluid, kinetic and ever-evolving. In organizing yourselves around static ideas and partial representations of Truth, you underestimate how much you are each personally loved and attended to. For again, because of Love, Truth is always evolving and growing to attend to Love's compassion for each individual and the needs of the time and place in which Truth's manifold aspects are in play. To relentlessly hold on to the same constructs of relative truths until they become stale and life-negating – whether through religious dogma, government constitutions or personal beliefs – is to corrupt and nullify the life-affirming Love that once gave those truths vitality and relevance.

We would wish for you each and all to be free from rigid notions about Truth that imprison your minds, exclude the truths of others and deny the greater knowings of your hearts. You will not fall off the edge of your world by re-examining the truths that you have continued to 'hold evident' and being willing to see that they are stepping stones to deeper and ever-evolving truths. For there are truths which you can know only at the altar of your own heart where the Divine meets you in a way that is utterly relevant to your particular life and soul, yet also connects you to the hearts, souls and truths of all others. Your truth is no less true when others do or don't abide by it. All truths reside within the wholeness of Truth, but there is no "only one truth" among you that does not need all of your pieces of truth, all of your love combined and commingled, in order to be wholly realized.

And thus, as long as humankind remains divisive within itself, you cannot be in possession of the whole Truth. But be not discouraged, for there will come a dawning on your planet when Love will prevail and swell among you to such heights that the whole Truth will be revealed in every heart and you will see and feel and know the Oneness that contains and includes the many individualities and expressions that you are.

In the meantime, through personal love and humility and in moments of meditation, prayer or contemplation, you can feel and even partake of the vastness of the All within the one you are as a kind of hologram, or 'tincture' of the whole Truth. This whole Truth, which will only be revealed on Earth by a critical mass of joined hearts, is the greater reality by which your group agreements and 'lesser' realities may be discerned and guided. In addition, it is only in the presence of Love and Truth in togetherness that true and loving justice will prevail. And it will be the kind of justice that does not seek retribution, but to balance all conditions of disharmony and disruption and restore what is life-affirming for all so that each may be free to be and express the love and truth of who you are.

Only in truth can each and all be free. Only in truth can freedom itself evolve to accommodate newly-emerging truths that enhance the whole. As truth sets you free, truth itself is set free to evolve into new and expanded truths. This of course is what some groups fear, because the group wants to protect the status quo and its reason for being. The key is for the group to realize that it too must grow so that it does not become a tyranny to its members and ultimately ineffective in its purposes. Be not afraid to re-examine your 'group agreements' from time to time, lest they stifle or even imprison the true becoming of individuals and thus weaken the group. For the true and lasting power of a group is in multiplying and magnifying individual power and purpose, not in maintaining the comfort of conformity.

Finally, dear one, draw from my MEBAHEL light to help you remember the most important thing about Truth in either its absolute or relative aspects – which is that no truth can be a whole truth without love. For truth may reveal the fact of someone's actions, but love tells the whole story of their intent and motivation, the purpose or pain that drives them. Think of this the next time you judge someone – or yourself – based on actions alone. As the fluidity of love tempers temporary fact or circumstance with mercy, compassion and understanding, what results is a healing justice of truth that no tradition or penal system can serve up. Every parent who has ever disciplined a dearly loved child understands this. Every truth that allows love and compassion to attend to what is needed in the moment proceeds from this. Dear uniquely wondrous one, be the love and truth you want to see in the world, that the world may be that much more ennobled, free and just because of you. Amen...

4/4 * 6/18 * 9/1 * 11/13 * **1/23**

15 HARIEL

(HA-ree-EL)

Purification (G)

'One who uses the light to wash clean'

Archangel ~ RAZIEL

Gemini / Mercury (6/1-5)

I AM THAT WHICH...

helps you to bring the purity which you hold in your heart, and your personal intentions and strivings, into your worldly creations, collaborations and organizations. Purity is a quality of being and doing that you bring to the world from the best of who you are and strive to be. Because there is so much fragmentation and 'disconnect' in your world among your personal, shared and public 'selves,' it is not uncommon for there to be purity in some aspects of your life and not in others. Indeed, there are many who espouse purity in their worldly endeavors and podiums as a hoped-for and even secret atonement for impure actions in their personal lives. But we wish you to realize that impurity on the personal level is a hidden 'spoiler' within all your worldly endeavors that can sooner or later contaminate your good works in the world. Few understand this better than the politicians and public figures with secret lives who are eventually exposed and toppled from their leadership and further aspirations, losing the respect of their peers and the public. Redemption, however, is usually possible with true remorse and the willingness to change.

Purity is born of a sense of truth which intends right action. It is not a strategy to be contrived or bartered. Your heart is the author of your purity, and once you connect on a feeling and wisdom level with this you can use your knowledge and experience to align your outer actions with your inner standard. We suggest that the oath of 'do no harm' which medical workers and healers strive to abide by is an excellent gauge for rightness and purity in all endeavors and engagements. How might your personal and public aspirations, business proposals, contractual relationships, citizen rights and global treaties change if 'do no harm' were part of the bottom line?

And so dear one I offer you my HARIEL light to realize more and more that a successful life is not about ***what*** *you accomplish or acquire in your world in terms of material benefits – but rather* ***how****. This is so very often exactly the reverse of your thinking and assuming, because much of your world values material success and regards the 'how' as a necessary 'whatever it takes' to get it. As we like to say again and again, in the microcosm of your personal world, as well as your interface with the greater world, you are all leaves on the same tree of life, each catching the light from your own unique angles. We promise that rather than letting the well-being of others fall by the wayside for personal self-interest and profit, you will be happiest if your methods and goals include the well-being of all. In truth, there is enough of everything to go around when the 'everything' is created and carried into the world with the creation energy of love. And the more you allow love to* ***possess you****, the more of everything you will have and be! Amen...*

4/5 * 6/19 * 9/2 * 11/14 * **1/24***

16 HAKAMIAH

(ha-KA-mee-YAH)

Loyalty (G)

'One who aligns with the inner Divine'

Archangel ~ RAZIEL

Gemini / Moon (6/6-10)

I AM THAT WHICH...

helps to inspire loyalty, harmony and cooperation with and among others through honorable and cohesive purpose and right action, and to integrate opposing ideas and factions in order to serve the highest good for each and all. Sooner or later and now and again, your endeavors in the world will call you to re-assess your loyalties. This is natural to the dualities of soul-body life in a world where both essence and form are always vying for power. You are so used to feeling fragmented and separated within yourself, however, that you can easily forget that both your soul and your body will have the most power if they work together as one. The same goes for how you work as an individual with the greater world of others in groups, organizations and governments. Any power or protocol that asks things of you that divide you within yourself, or pits your interests against those of others, will create a crisis of loyalty. When this happens, you will need to remember what matters most in your life and true purpose – and unless that 'most' is something more profound than money, position or power, then you will remain divided and torn no matter what you choose.

And so dear one, I bring unto you my HAKAMIAH light that you might better see and embrace what you truly and lovingly value, and to renew your remembrance of this whenever your loyalty is called 'to task.' Cultivate a heart within you which listens to the whispers of your soul – because therein will be a wisdom for your own life that only you have access to. Let you be loyal to such a heart within you, and you will know how to balance your worldly loyalties. For when you are loyal to what truly matters, matter without meaning will become a lesser and lesser god among you. Amen...

* Governs 1/24 simultaneously with 17 LAVIAH.

January 24 – 31

Angels 17 – 24

Sephira 3

BINAH ~ Understanding

Overlighting Archangel

TZAPHKIEL ~ 'Beholder of the Divine'
Understanding of self and God, contemplation, meditation and compassion

---

17 LAVIAH
18 CALIEL
19 LEUVIAH
20 PAHALIAH
21 NELCHAEL
22 YEIAYEL
23 MELAHEL
24 HAHEUIAH

4/6 * 6/20 * 9/3 * 11/15 * **1/24***

17 LAVIAH

(LAH-vee-YAH)

Revelation (R)

'One who parts the veil'

Archangel ~ TZAPHKIEL

Gemini / Uranus (6/11-15)

I AM THAT WHICH...

fosters an ability to 'walk in two worlds' in search of ways to bring the stuff of Heaven to Earth in order to elevate your experience of life and inspire others to their own higher potentials. Revelation in your world in its utmost display is about revealing the spiritual, or 'super-reality' which, albeit seemingly 'hidden,' co-exists with and sustains your material reality. Thus revelation is always about showing something that is already here but which perhaps has not yet been seen or realized. Many of your religious and spiritual traditions and teachings are founded on 'revelations' by prophets, teachers, gurus and those who are deemed to be 'anointed' or holy. But as many of these extraordinary beings have affirmed, what they have done, 'you can do, and more.'

Anything you desire to be revealed is accessible to you by bringing your presence to the present, which is time's door into the eternal. Through this door the essential energies of all things and beings reside and are knowable. As esoteric as this may sound, for many of you experiences of revelation occur daily during activities as varied as creativity, meditation, walking or working in nature – to sleeping or dreaming, bathing and toiletry! The key is ***immersion*** *into whatever you are doing in the moment in a way that allows concerns of this world to be suspended so that you can* *'hear' the voices of the 'other-worlds' which come through your soul, or what you call 'higher self', into your heart and mind.*

One of the powerful ways that revelations are broadcast from within you unto the world is through the creative arts – such as art, music, poetry and other kinds of writing. When you engage in creativity of any kind for the love of it, seeking to bring the truth of it forward, you are reprising the first act of creation that brought life itself into being from itself, and thus you endow your creations with that same creation energy. This is why great works of art, thought, feeling and wisdom have such a long 'shelf-life' in your world – because you are re-enlivened by the creation energy those works carry, the truths they reveal and the depths of greater-knowing that often lie dormant within your hearts until something provocative stirs you awake to what is beautiful and deep in yourselves that you forgot was there.

And so dear you who have the power to see, feel and know with faculties infinitely beyond the senses of your body and mind – I invite you to partake of my LAVIAH light to immerse your doing self into the focus and inspiration of beingness. Thus may you be awake to the 'in-spiriting' of the eternal otherness that dwells and creates through you and with you from within you. Relax your heart from the clench of mind and world so that you may receive and co-create what mind and world so deeply need. And bless you for bringing the wholeness, and the holiness, of your co-creations as a light unto all. Amen...

* Governs 1/24 simultaneously with 16 HAKAMIAH

4/7 * 6/21 * 9/4 * 11/16 * **1/25**

18 CALIEL

(KA-lee-EL)

Justice (S)

'One who sustains the cosmic laws of love and truth for all'

Archangel ~ TZAPHKIEL

Gemini / Saturn (6/16-21)

I AM THAT WHICH...

helps to reveal the dynamics and causes of injustice, and to cultivate your realization that only love, understanding and compassion can restore justice among you. Injustice begets more of the same. The same will hold true for the reverse when you begin to redefine justice in your individual consciousness, and thus ultimately in your diverse cultures and communities. An original, causal injustice can fuel ongoing injustices for generations by the lack of historical hindsight about original cause. For example, a people's homeland can be seized by a conquering invader in one century, and many centuries later when the original inhabitants take back their land, the current inhabitants see it as an unjust disenfranchisement of what has been their homeland for centuries. There is a tendency in the temporal nature of Earth-life to be so focused on getting what you want right now that you do not realize the consequences to others in your present and future world.

In the natural cosmic law that restores balance over time by allowing all things and beings to reap whatever is sown – therefore if you want to reap a different fruit, you must sow a different seed. There is no cure in revenge and retribution, only more dishonor and disenfranchisement of your inner Divine heritage and your greater human powers. As long as you mistake punishment or revenge for justice, you will only beget more injustice. The cure for injustice is neither of these, but rather it is the surrender of fear, hate and blame to the healing powers of love, compassion and forgiveness that bring true and lasting justice in a way that is rehabilitative and life-affirming for all.

Thus, I give you my light-justice as CALIEL, that you who have ever felt infringed upon unjustly may look to the history of your own actions and those of your people – even unto the generations – to see where it all began. Be the link that stops the cycles of reaction in the long chain of unjust actions. For the only true honor is the honor of the heart that conveys love and compassion, and the 'other cheek' which is turned to allow one last act of injustice from which there will be no more need of sacrifice. All beings are equal in their preciousness to the Originator of life, for there is nothing or no one that is not made of Love. To understand this as the equalness of worth that underlies all diversities of race, creed, color and emotional, mental and physical capacities is to understand that true justice is truly 'for one and all.'

Thus the end of injustice is the beginning of love – the great dissolver of fear, blame, anger and hatred. It all starts and comes back to you and him and her and each and all as individuals. Be just. Be love. And the being of one multiplied into the many will accomplish the doing among you. Amen...

4/8 * 6/22 * 9/5 * 11/17 * **1/26**

19 LEUVIAH

(LOO-vee-YAH)

Expansive Intelligence & Fruition (G)

'One who uses heart to quicken soul memory and expand mind'

Archangel ~ TZAPHKIEL

Cancer / Jupiter (6/22-26)

I AM THAT WHICH...

helps you to draw from collective memory and the wisdom of your own life passages, as well as of the generations, to make a great work of your life in the present time. A sense of history is important – not to keep things as they 'always were,' but to carry forward what you've learned in order to evolve individual and collective intelligence and the capacity to bring higher ideals into tangible fruition. Like the warm sun that compels the seed to push through the dark soil to light and life, it is depth of feeling and trueness of cause that give dreams, ideas and goals the thrust that can propel them, and you, into the ongoingness of time. Today is yesterday's hope and tomorrow's history, but in the meantime today is your eternity. Today, in the eternal now of the present, you have the power to bring forth the sweetest fruit from even the bitter seeds of yesterday. And that power resides in your heart, through the alchemy of love and wisdom that can transform the least into the most, what wasn't into what is and who you were not into who you are now.

Perhaps the greatest mystery of life is the paradoxical nature of Divine-Human beingness – in which life is a creative 'stage' where you may perform the magic of what more is humanly possible when you tap into the non-limitation of your Divine soul at the altar of a passionate heart. Remarkable achievement is more than skill, experience or education. It is a doing that comes from what you call the 'fire in your belly,' the dream in your heart or the longing in your soul – and your own heart leaps in recognition every time you witness it in the world. It happens when people do the impossible, when hope is found within hopeless situations, when the only way 'to get there from here' is with a leap of faith. Such a way is always rooted in truth and moved by love.

No matter what you did or did not do yesterday, you and all of humankind have another first chance every new day of your lives. Thus, dear one, draw from my LEUVIAH light that you may tap the unlimited resources of the Divine to sail beyond the illusory limitations of your humanity. 'Imagine all the people' doing the impossible together. Deepening thought with feeling, expanding mind with heart, transforming the whole world with love. So may it be. And we promise you, it will someday, in a new present time of your own making. Amen...

4/9 * 6/23 * 9/6 * 11/18 * **1/27**

20 PAHALIAH

(pa-HA-lee-AH)

Redemption (G)

'One who restores the self'

Archangel ~ TZAPHKIEL

Cancer / Mars (6/27-7/1)

I AM THAT WHICH...

seeds in the collective heart of humankind the understanding that true 'salvation' is about the realization that all of you, without exception, are manifested expressions of Divine Love and Truth – and that the reclaiming of yourselves as such does not come through dogma and belief systems, but through the graces of the heart. There are many among you who wait for the first or second coming of 'the Messiah.' But as long as you think your God and your 'salvation' are outside you, or available to some and not others, you shall not come into your Divine-Human fullness and truly thrive. We ask you to consider this: ***the true redeemer of humankind shall come from within you and among you and shall be called Love****. For only Love and the graces of compassion and forgiveness can restore you to awareness of your inner Divinity and the biases of mind and matter with a language that every heart understands and quickens to. Only Love can go 'where none have gone before' to create healing and peace. Only Love can reveal the Truth that you are brother-and-sister souls born from Love, made of Love and therefore always 'saved' by Love.*

Throughout your histories many have come to tell you these things – and while your hearts have been stirred, you have had the need to organize your realizations and experiences into doctrine, dogma and ritual. These are helpful when used to create an atmosphere in which you may return to and re-enliven the heart of the teachings. But because the feeling experience of Love and Truth can be elusive when you are not utterly present, and your world is so full of distractions and busyness, you have learned to identify with 'outer trappings' and practices. We do not tell you to do away with your traditions, but rather to go deeper into the heart of them wherein it is revealed that your saving Love is not fixed but fluid, not exclusive but inclusive, and not the possession of any one dogma but the fulfillment of them all.

And thus dear seeking one, I offer you my PAHALIAH light of redemption to see that you are already 'saved' because you are made of the very Love that already saves you – again and again. Through Love you can know this whole paradoxical truth of yourself and of all creation: you each and all are here to create and experience the endlessly diverse ways in which flesh and bone, matter and form, time and place can be transformed and infinitely increased through Divine Love – the Love that ever lives and breathes within and among you, for you and as you. Amen...

4/10 * 6/24 * 9/7 * 11/19 * **1/28**

21 NELCHAEL

(NEL-ka-EL)

Ardent Desire to Learn (G)

'One who inspires delight in learning'

Archangel ~ TZAPHKIEL

Cancer / Sun (7/2-6)

I AM THAT WHICH...

fosters in you an enthusiasm to learn about the ways of others who are not of your 'tribe,' so that you might appreciate the contributions of their differences, as well as the commonalities you share. It is usual to be drawn to people who are similar to you, with similar backgrounds, values and belief systems. Familiarity brings a sense of safety and comfort, making it easier to get on with your busy lives. However, you can get so comfortable with what and who you know that you miss the gifts of the unknown that await you around every corner of the known left behind – just as you did when you left the womb for the world.

One of the things you most delight in about your young children is their delight in learning. As they gain a sense of personal safety and independence through walking and talking, their sphere of awareness and curiosity widens. If their sensibilities are not limited by adult preferences and biases, their curiosities are especially triggered by things and beings that are different from their everyday exposures and experiences. For the 'young and impressionable,' every word, deed and experience is a learning seed that will gestate within them and be cultivated over time, for better or worse. If they are encouraged to be interested in that which is 'different' or new, while they also learn discernment using their own instincts and intuitions, then their experience of living will be rooted in curiosity and enthusiasm rather than fear and suspicion. Would you not want that for your children? Would you not want that for yourself?

And so let us talk about church and state. In the parts of the world where these have been 'separated,' it has helped to prevent the religious persecution of centuries past. However, it has also prevented people learning about each others' ways and traditions – and so persecution still continues through fear-based attitudes, social bias and violence. If you include the learning of all traditions in your educational systems rather than excluding them, you will create opportunities for learning about each other, and these will be the seeds for understanding that will go beyond tolerance into appreciation – and eventually, yes, world peace.

Therefore is my NELCHAEL light given to help you realize that the differences among you are your potential strengths when you are willing to learn and see their value to the whole. For each of you carries a seed of knowledge and a piece of truth, and each of you are expressing a unique angle of Divine Light and Beingness as only you can. If you want to know the whole Truth, then you must, with love, learn about the pieces that others hold and express. Indeed, it is only with love that you can learn not only what is apparent, but what is hidden – not only what is different, but what is at the heart of all the same. And so dear ones, open your hearts and learn who you are to each other, and that with each other you can be so much more. Amen...

4/11 * 6/25 * 9/8 * 11/20 * **1/29**

22 YEIAYEL

(YAY-ah-YEL)

Fame, Renown (G)

'One who seeks knowing of self'

Archangel ~ TZAPHKIEL

Cancer / Venus (7/7-11)

I AM THAT WHICH...

helps you to use personal success as a podium for inspiration and service to community and the world. As more and more of you who enjoy fame and celebrity are aware, renown is a planet-wide podium from which to inspire and impact the greater good. But famous or not, every one of you is a walking, talking, word-in-action – whether through charismatic persuasions, visionary inspirations and deeds, expository truths and challenges or remarkable acts of love and compassion. In your age of boundless technology, anyone and everyone can be famous to the person next door thousands of miles away. What do you want to say with your podium? What effect do you want to create in the hearts and minds of others? How do you want to contribute to the evolution of consciousness in your personal and public realms?

In your world, the well-being of the whole needs collectives of individuals to work together who embody and pursue life-affirming values and goals. In the bigger picture of life, each of you is vital to filling in the full spectrum of textures, themes, colors, timbres, meanings and other qualities ad infinitum that the Bigger Picture has envisioned for itself and for you. And you are vital to each other because in collaboration each makes the other more than either could be on your own. Thus together you are each co-creating your world and contributing to the quality of life for all.

In some families, groups and communities, individuals are constrained to walk the middle road and not be too 'different' or stand out in order to satisfy misconceived ideals of humility. Often where these constraints prevail, individuation and excellence may languish, and the community will ultimately be weakened as those who have 'bigger dreams' leave for places that do not limit achievement. In other communities where success and fame are over-idealized, substance and meaning can be under-valued as actions are undertaken for the sole purpose of attention or immediate gain. But the individual heart and soul wants more, and so does the soul of the world need that more, which you have the intrinsic power to bring to it.

My YEIAYEL light is given so that you might become an inspiration and light to others – not so that they might follow you, but that you might create awareness that each one has a unique light within themselves. Be the match that lights the candle, enabling that candle to light the next, which will light another and so on, until there is a magnificence of everyone's light shining forth to be seen, known and cherished by all. So be it in your hearts and in the world, in loving and true time. Amen...

4/12 * 6/26 * 9/9 * 11/21 * **1/30**

23 MELAHEL

(MAY-la-HEL)

Healing Capacity (G)

'One who shows where healing is possible'

Archangel ~ TZAPHKIEL

Cancer / Mercury (7/12-16)

I AM THAT WHICH...

helps to provide an atmosphere in which mutual understanding and compassion become resources for empathy, healing and a new sense of unity. Healing of any kind happens naturally when the environment is conducive for it. In any eruption of hurt, there must be a willingness to address not only the immediate cause, but original cause and all contributing factors. When you do this not as a 'witch-hunt' for blame, but to better understand all that must be healed, that which is hurting will show itself.

It is natural to want to distance yourself from the discomfort of the discovery process, but no one is truly exempt from contributing to either healing or harm in your world. Each of you plays a part according to your unique nature and what you carry within you. To point fingers of blame to one does not exempt any other. Indeed, it is not an issue of blame, but the willingness to open your heart to participate in the world's healing through your own awareness, compassion and sense of humane responsibility.

Thus, I offer my MELAHEL light to help you see through the eyes of your heart that you are interconnected with your fellow beings and the Earth itself – for you are all sprung from the same Source, and the essence and energy of that Source is contained within and shared by all of you, with no exceptions. It is natural to become disheartened by all the violence and chaos in your world –

but when violence erupts or a 'bad' thing happens, may you see that the event is showing you where healing is needed – in the same way symptoms help to show where your physical, mental or emotional body is sick.

Therefore, let you not judge or be judged, but seek healing for yourself and each other in the big or small ways you are each called to. Smile at your neighbor to lift her day. Speak kindly to all you meet. Notice those who live alone in your community and offer to help. For love of your Earth, pick up a piece of trash someone else has thrown on the ground, or dare to take a stand against the ravaging and misuse of her resources. Put away apathy to feel what there is to feel and be willing to heal and be healed. Simply, be willing to love, and all the rest will come. Amen...

4/13 * 6/27 * 9/10 * 11/22 * **1/31**

24 HAHEUIAH

(ha-HOO-ee-YAH)

Protection (G)

'One who is the keeper of true-selfness'

Archangel ~ TZAPHKIEL

Cancer / Moon (7/17-22)

I AM THAT WHICH...

fosters the realization that you are each other's protectors – guardians not only of your mutual right to fulfill your purposes, desires and well-being at every level, but also guardians of the Earth and all her creatures. Each species on Earth comes into being in order to express the unique potential of itself through the natural seasons and cycles of change which move all of life forward. On your Earth, only you have the sophisticated abilities to think and feel deeply, to process patterns and purposes, to envision and achieve, to communicate and commune, to discern meaning and command the essence and energies of life. But you can be in true and full dominion only when you realize that with great ability and power comes great responsibility and care towards those with seemingly lesser or different powers.

In all the millennia of human existence, few have fully understood and respected that all beings of the natural world have sentience and their own languages of thinking, feeling and communication. Just because you may not have the wherewithal to understand the ways of these or any doesn't mean that they are inferior to your kind. Each and every being and thing possesses the intrinsic nobility of their own isness as a diverse and unique expression of the Divine 'I Am.' And all are here not only to expand the Divine on Earth through the fulfillment of their beingness, but also to serve each other in doing so.

Thus dear greatly endowed one, use my HAHEUHIAH light to help you respect and protect each other's cultures and habitats rather than trying to control, conquer or change them to your ways. In an age wherein technology has made the world smaller, conditions of your farthest neighbors are more easily known. You are all watching and being influenced by each other. Therefore, affirm life in your own cultures and become examples of respect, kindness and caring. Do not force others to your ways, but invite them to the best of their own life-affirming potentials.

And look to the day when you will not want to take creatures out of their natural habitats in order to study their magnificence, only to realize too late that they wither in confinement. Value the lives of animals more than your profit from their parts and the trinkets and exotic, unnecessary or even unhealthy foods which their deaths provide to your marketplace. Respect and love your Earth as a living sentient being – indeed as the mother, guardian, teacher and supplier of all in this your home away from Home – for her diminishment would also be your own.

And especially, dear ones, protect your inner humanity – what is true and loving and sacred in yourselves and each other – so that together you might come to understand the whole truth about the mysteries of life and love. Amen...

February 1 – 8

Angels 25 – 32

Sephira 4

CHESED ~ Love/Mercy

Overlighting Archangel

TZADKIEL ~ 'Justice of God'
Mercy and kindness, beneficence,
grace, transmutation

---

25 NITH-HAIAH
26 HAAIAH
27 YERATEL
28 SEHEIAH
29 REIYEL
30 OMAEL
31 LECABEL
32 VASARIAH

4/14 * 6/28 * 9/11 * 11/23 * **2/1**

25 NITHAIAH

(NIT-ha-YAH)

Spiritual Wisdom and Magic (R)

'One who quickens the abracadabra of life'

Archangel ~ TZADKIEL

Leo / Uranus (7/23-27)

I AM THAT WHICH...

helps you to cultivate an enthusiastic relationship with esoteric mysteries and to become an inspired conductor of spiritual wisdom and the magic of life with the loving, living energies of the heart. The true magic of spiritual play in life happens when you are met by something 'beyond' in the here and now in a way that most personally speaks to you. When we say 'something beyond,' we do not speak of only the discarnate Divine, Angels, guides and 'heavenly signs and wonders' – but the ability of your own soul-powered hearts to create spiritual magic in each other's lives. When you transcend your outer differences to connect with each other on the inside, sparks of recognition are fired and you get that magical feeling of a destined moment or meeting that makes you feel known by the other – and even by the universe itself.

The ability to convey your unique wisdom and 'larger-than-life' magic unto the world starts with your willingness to experience the depths of your own being and the magic of your ongoing becoming. You are naturally oriented toward life from your dominant qualities, interests, passions and talents – which may be particularly expressed through any and all of your parts. As a 'four-part' being composed of soul, heart, mind and body, the part of you which speaks most directly, wisely and 'magically' to others is your heart. Love and wisdom, the two greatest resources of your heart, are universal languages. Those who are often held in high esteem among you – those who have 'that something extra' – are those whose inner heart-fire inspires their talents and offerings to transcend technique, skill or knowledge. You recognize this instantly by the soaring of your own heart in watching an extraordinary performance or presentation of any kind. As when a dancer or skater seems to leap skyward with uncommon passion or grace, or an athlete's against-all-odds performance brings him across the finish line first – or last. You see it in the prevailing of the underdog and a child who smiles at a stranger that others ignore or abhor. You hear it in the words of someone who speaks a more whole truth that only love can know, or in the mutual respect of two people who recognize the humanity in each other despite their warring factions.

I, NITHAIAH, assure you that by virtue of the love, generosity, humility, compassion and intuition of your heart, you have the power to lift each other up and be reminded of your innate wisdom and personal truths. Only with your hearts may you know the other's, only with your hearts may you meet at your sameness within while enjoying your differences. Only with your hearts may you open closed minds, move immoveable mountains or turn the tide in an oncoming sea of strife. Only with your hearts may you change a wayward world. Amen...

4/15 * 6/29 * 9/12 * 11/24 * **2/2**

26 HAAIAH

(HA-ee-YAH)

Political Science and Ambition (R)

'One who encourages cooperative expression'

Archangel ~ TZADKIEL

Leo / Saturn (7/28-8/1)

I AM THAT WHICH...

helps to purify and repurpose ambition to advance a more humane and beneficent world order based on the values of the heart and the cosmic order of Divine Love and Truth which intends that all beings should come into full expression of their true nature and highest good. You come to Earth to develop and advance your own unique being and purposes – but this is not your 'endgame.' Your ultimate soul-desire is that your own greater becoming will give you a greaterness to offer to the world. Anything you create in your world that is love-life-and-light-affirming advances that greaterness for yourself as well as others. When your individual ambitions are aligned with this 'soul-standard,' and you bring these personal values to your workplace and community endeavors, there is no end to the ripple effect of possibility that you will have set into motion throughout the Earth and the Heavens.

All things in your world can be used to accomplish good for yourself and others. The most beneficent potential of a political system is to organize the collective of individual ambitions into a value system of opportunity and good for all. But in the duality that is the context of Earth life, the fruit of ambition will turn either sweet or sour according to the soil that nurtures it. Thus, the energies of politics and ambition are 'good,' or life-affirming, if they are life-advancing not only for you – but also for others. And when we say 'others,' we do not mean a closed or exclusive society or group, but open to all who are desirous to partake and contribute. It is not enough to build a family 'dynasty' without also contributing to society as a whole. You have a saying, 'to whom much is given, much is expected.' Power should never be used to deprive anyone of that which you desire for yourself, and the truly powerful individual is one who can also help to empower others.

I shine my HAAIAH light within and upon you so that you might use ambition rightly among you. Corruption is a symptom of your natural beneficence being forgotten, suppressed or distorted. Corruption revealed is a 'call to action' to all, not just corporations and governments. It is an opportunity to remember what you truly value and to set about reinstating that in the what, why and how of what you do. Just as corruption often begins with the acts of one individual, so must the rehabilitation of corruption begin with the willingness of individuals, carried forth into community. What can one person do? When you look at what you are doing or not doing, dear one, look with the seeing of your heart and you will know what you can do, indeed, what ***only you*** *can do. Amen...*

4/16 + 17am * 6/30 * 9/13 * 11/25 * **2/3**

27 YERATEL

(YEH-ra-TEL)

Propagation of the Light (S)

'One who grows the light with love'

Archangel ~ TZADKIEL

Leo / Jupiter (8/2-6)

I AM THAT WHICH...

helps to cultivate the power and purpose of light within your choices, creations, endeavors and organizations in order to awaken hearts and minds to higher ideals and actions. Light is one of the most pervasive aspects of human life. It is also foundational to your existence, because it is the very stuff your soul is made of! In your earthly realm, you understand the phenomenon of light as either naturally sourced from the sun, moon, stars, certain insect or sea species, and so on – or mechanically sourced by harnessing natural forces such as fire, wind, water and more as electrical catalysts and conductivity. You also speak of light in your metaphors, deeper-meanings and spiritual realms – such as 'the light of day,' 'the light of truth,' 'the light of love,' 'the light of understanding,' 'the light of the Spirit,' 'the light of Creation,' and such. And you sometimes describe each other as having a light, or glow, about you. In the cosmic realms, we understand light as the very fabric of creation, composed of the commingled isness of Divine Truth and the warmth and energy-in-motion of Divine Love which expands Truth.

In the duality of Earth-life, you are composed of both light and dark – the light of love and truth held within your soul which is always broadcasting to your heart, as well as the dark and denser humus of the Earth that forms your physicality and gives your soul 'a leg to stand on.' As such you are a walking talking Divine-Human paradox with the right to choose which of your aspects you will draw from at any moment of your life. 'Light-consciousness' enables you to grow the light within you by becoming aware of and interacting with it. As your inner light expands, all your human aspects, including your body, are lightened and enlightened – even unto the 'ascension' of your consciousness while you are still in the body.

You come to Earth to experience the full spectrum of humanness. However, when you become conscious of your inner Divine light and allow it to illuminate and ennoble your humanity, you become 'a light unto the world' shining the magnificence of what is possible when you fully embrace your Divine-Human nature.

Thus my Light as YERATEL dwells within you to amplify and grow your Divine soul-light in your heart, mind and body. Through light, all things are possible in your own life and in the world. It is on Earth and in your human heart where the Divine Heart comes to put down roots of love and truth. Thus, let my light awaken your greater understanding that you and the Earth are co-creators and proliferators of the light you are made of at your very essence. Be light, individually and together, that your hearts, humanity, the Earth and the Divine within you, may all blossom. Amen...

4/17pm + 18 * 7/1 * 9/14 * 11/26 * **2/4**

28 SEHEIAH

(say-HAY-ee-YAH)

Longevity (G)

'One who extends life with creation energy'

Archangel ~ TZADKIEL

Leo / Mars (8/7-12)

I AM THAT WHICH...

helps you to revitalize and sustain enthusiasm for what you contribute to community and collaboration by stoking the fires of inspiration for new creations, while also allowing situations, things and people to gestate and unfold in the flow of their time. Your longevity and joy as a creator and contributor to your world is intimately connected to your willingness to grow what you love in the cyclical flow of life and regeneration. You must say yes to life in order to renew life! Saying yes by immersing yourself in what you love will open the doors of inspiration that allow you to be a creator 'from the school of' the Divine Itself.

What you love will always love you back, but often in ways very different than what you think you want or expect. For your love, which is an expression of the Divine Love that dwells within your soul, will give you what you need and save you again and again from whatever you might need saving from! Each time you bring your love to the world, you are helping to save it. For love in action is love awake, and the presence of awakened love has the power to wake love in the hearts and minds of all.

And so, to live long in your world – whether in your own physicality, your creations or in the hearts and minds of those who go on without you – is to love long and deep and wide. Love, and resist not. Welcome and engage with what is true and utterly relevant to you and what you desire to give. Do not resist that which is not, but rather simply do not engage. For when you engage with what is not life-affirming for you, even to fight against it for a noble cause, you vibrate at the level of that which you fight. Rather, hold space for what you love, what you affirm and desire to increase. In this there is no stress, no 'dominion of death,' but only rejuvenation, renewal and rebirth.

These same principles apply in your relationship to the Earth itself and any societies in which you desire to make a long-lasting positive contribution. To sacrifice long-term well-being for short-term gain is the death of sustainable profit at every level. If you must cut a tree to build a house, then plant a new tree. If you must destroy a home to build a new road – or a hundred new homes – then provide a new home-place to the displaced, at the very least. If you must take anything away, give something back that will yield more than what was taken. Do not force success, but do your part for the whole, even without accolades or recognition.

I, SEHEIAH, remind you that you are co-creators with your Earth and each other. The longevity of the Earth, your kind, and all, depend on the acts of your heart that come not from temporal desires, but eternal values. Do these things not only for your children and theirs, but for the soul of you that will come again and again to experience the marvel of life as an embodied spark of the Divine's great desire to know life as only you can live and love it. Amen...

4/19 * 7/2 * 9/15 * 11/27 * **2/5**

29 REIYEL

(RAY-ee-YEL)

Liberation (G)

'One who liberates the love and truth of you'

Archangel ~ TZADKIEL

Leo / Sun (8/13-17)

I AM THAT WHICH...

helps you to be a 'lightning rod' for illuminating greater truths and providing pathways, platforms and conduits that allow you to be free to choose your own way according to your true calling. No person, group or situation can ever truly imprison you if your first belonging is to the Divine that dwells within you as your own soul-light. That said, we understand the deep need to belong that drives so many private actions, societal organizations and religious affiliations. Fear of unbelonging stems from an underlying sense of being exiled from your 'true homeland' – the eternal essence that is the Source of your soul nature. Thus, as refugees leaving their home country congregate together in a new land, you create 'pods' of familiarity and belonging by cohabiting and affiliating with people who seem to be of your tribe in culture or creed in order to feel more at home. While this can be comforting and supportive, when groups and belief systems become exclusive of other worldviews and ways they can become constrictive to individual and societal growth. This exclusivity can ultimately become a kind of prison that locks you into what is considered by the group to be acceptable thought, behavior and associations. In effect, the group agreement becomes your 'lesser god,' chipping away at the true God within you which desires nothing less for you than the freedom to be and express who you truly are.

In order to be truly free and allow truth itself to be free to grow and evolve you into new beingness, we wish for you to know this: Any truth you may know or follow is only a half-truth without Love, and your own beliefs and experiences of Truth are only a relative particle of the totality of Truth itself. For all of you are so loved that Truth comes to each of you in a way that you may best understand and engage with it. The way home to your personal truth is always through your heart, and thus 'there are as many roads leading home as hearts willing to come.' If you want to know if any truth is a 'true truth,' ask yourself this: Does it free or imprison? Does it expand love or fear?

And so we say as the light of REIYEL together with all the diverse Angelic hues of the Divine within your 'hue-manity:' wherever lies your belonging in your world, let it be such that you are free to engage with the different ways love and truth express through your heart and also in the hearts of others. For here in the heart, where the Divine meets the Human, is humankind's innermost altar of salvation and the keeper of your freedom. So go forth dear one and be free, as you free our light to dwell within and among you, each and all. Amen...

4/20 * 7/3 * 9/16 * 11/28 * **2/6**

30 OMAEL

(O-ma-EL)

Fertility, Multiplicity (G)

'One who loves life into being'

Archangel ~ TZADKIEL

Leo / Venus (8/18-22)

I AM THAT WHICH...

helps you to plant new and different seeds of love and light in your creations, endeavors and collaborations so that you may harvest a sweeter and more nourishing fruit. One of the great laws of life pervasive throughout the ages and generations of living things and beings is 'whatsoever you sow, that shall you reap.' As individuals you are each a seed in the totality of humanity and its creations. What kind of seed are you in the different moments of your hours and days? What kinds of seeds do you scatter and plant as you talk and walk through your world? Are you aware that your very presence and every word you speak and thing you do seeds the beginning of a creation in your world? Just as a bitter seed will not yield a sweet fruit, neither will a bitter word yield a sweet response. However, because of the power of your heart to change the past and the future by what you do with the present, you can transform and multiply anything that seems to be life-limiting or negating into something that is life-affirming and generative.

This is what you do when you choose to 'turn the other cheek' instead of taking 'an eye for an eye.' For when you turn you have a chance to see with a different perspective – but if any keep taking an eye for an eye, soon the whole world may be blinded. When 'bad' things happen, look to the source, the beginning action that caused this terrible ripple – even generations later – instead of reacting in kind or becoming disheartened or angry, as if it has nothing to do with you. You may not be personally at blame in this life, but you can be personally responsible. You have the power to plant different seeds, and together with others you can plant enough of them to displace the weeds of the past that would encroach upon the fruit of the future.

And so, even while your world seems to be running amuck with dangers and disasters, prepare a more nutritive soil within heart and mind for the light-seeds of new becoming. Use my OMAEL light of fertility in the 'winter seasons' of these endeavors, when new beginnings are still gestating, to be attentive at more subtle, even hidden, levels. Love the thing you desire to bring into being even before you know what it is – and thus have faith that the love you bring to its gestation will yield love, sooner or later, in one form or another. This is how you plant yourself as a light-seed within your communities and your world, one person at a time, multiplied into many, times the many more.

There is no power greater than love because everything is made of love, and love is naturally drawn to itself for its own proliferation. Therefore love cannot be defeated, no matter how 'beat down' it may seem at times. 'So go forth and multiply' love so that truth may grow in the heaven-on-earth of human hearts everywhere. Amen...

4/21 * 7/4 + 5am * 9/17 * 11/29 * **2/7**

31 LECABEL

(LAY-ka-BEL)

Intellectual Talent (G)

'One who puts all the pieces together'

Archangel ~ TZADKIEL

Virgo / Mercury (8/23-28)

I AM THAT WHICH...

helps you to cultivate a visionary ability to combine the unique talents, skills and intelligences of diverse people and resources in order to bring about extraordinary achievement. Your world needs visionaries – those who see the bigger picture in each piece and each piece in the bigger picture, those who know what only the wisdom of the heart can reveal, and those who feel what others truly need beyond the grasping of greed or want. Such a see-er understands the profound importance of diversity at all levels, and at the same time knows how to harness the power of unity by weaving together the threads of sameness within the hearts of all. You too can be a visionary in your own life just by your willingness to see.

Everything each of you are, do, express and create helps to manifest on Earth an aspect of the greatest paradox of all – the inherent diversity of the Divine Oneness. And it takes all of you to make up the spirit, heart, mind and body of the Divine on Earth. Some of you particularly express the spirit of the divine, some more of the Divine Heart, some Divine Mind, and still others the wonder of Divine Being rendered in beautiful proportions and performance of physicality. To have the intellectual talent to see this is to recognize how the patterns and purposes of the eternal realms can be played out and expanded in time and place through collaboration and cooperation. By embracing the wonders of all your differences as vital to the functioning and well-being of the whole, together you can make a difference in your world.

You are each other's most precious resources. If you want to know what God is, take in the wonder of the other within you and beside you – for 'where two or more are gathered, there shall I be.' I invite you to use my LECABEL light to see that in all peoples and purposes, you will find me in my potential as you. Here I am, and here you are, in the garbage collector who helps to lighten your life by carting off things no longer needed – in the hairdresser who lightens your heart with listening as she lightens or cuts your hair – in the mailman who brings you reminders of your earthly connections and responsibilities – in the plumber who restores flow to some of your life's vital functions – in the homeless person on the street who gives you a chance to feel compassion – in business owners, leaders and organizations who, at their best, serve not only as touchstones for your higher aspirations, but at their 'worst' as clarions for what needs healing in your preoccupations and priorities.

It is the visionary capacity of a talented intellect to discern the value in all things and people and bring them together. And still, your blind spot is another person's vantage point. Work together, and together you will be all-seeing. Amen...

4/22 * 7/5pm + 6 * 9/18 * 11/30 * **2/8**

32 VASARIAH

(va-SAH-ree-YAH)

Clemency and Equilibrium (G)

'One who balances judgment with mercy'

Archangel ~ TZADKIEL

Virgo / Moon (8/29-9/2)

I AM THAT WHICH...

helps to cultivate community responsibility for individual transgressions and the loving compassion and mercy that can reform both the offender and the community more profoundly than punishment. There are many ways in which humans transgress and infringe upon each other. But when you view a transgression through the eyes of your heart, you will often see that behind the masks of desperation, anger, greed, belligerence, resentment, cruelty and such is simply this: someone in pain who is secretly longing to be loved and healed, in a community that also needs healing. To punish the act without striving to heal the actor and his context is only to 'add grease to a hot frying pan' and escalate the possibility for more transgression. Without transformation there is no true reform of the behavioral reactions and thought processes that result in harm to self and others. We look forward to the day when you realize that like water and wind against stone, only love and mercy can reshape hardened hearts and minds – and also turn the harboring of blame into a sense of communal awareness and response-ability.

There is a tendency to treat offenders as if they are different from you and to isolate them from the rest of society. However, because you are truly diverse expressions of an underlying Oneness, a hurt within one ripples out energetically and affects the collective psyche of all beings, including the Earth itself. Wherever communities harbor disproportionate conditions and disenfranchised peoples – and especially in cities where the 'haves and have-nots' are living in close proximity – frustration, anger, resentment and blame fester. And so we say, learn to view offenders as pointers to what needs healing among you.

When hurts and disturbances are suppressed in individuals or collectives, they do not go away. Rather they fester to a 'critical mass' of emotional and energetic momentum that will naturally seek an exit place to 'pop' and 'let off steam.' Like the eruption of boiling lava from a volcano, or of rashes on the skin due to an imbalanced condition in the body, societal 'boiling points' will often focalize in one or more people in a community who suddenly commit some kind of transgression or atrocity against others. When this occurs, if you can get beyond blaming the offender to see the seeds of the offense within distorted conditions somewhere in the community, then you have a real chance for communal rehabilitation and healing.

And so I invite you to use my VASARIAH mercy-light that dwells within your hearts to see in every offense the call for healing needed and possible among you all. You are sisters and brothers, and many of you are in pain. Do not look away, do not run away, but rather attend to the pain of the other, who is also yourself, and you will be shown a path that you can walk together for healing. Amen...

February 9 – 16

Angels 33 – 40

Sephira 5

GEBURAH ~ Strength & Judgment

Overlighting Archangel

CHAMAEL ~ 'Severity of God'
(Also CHAMUEL or KAMAEL)
Change, purification and clearing of karma
for stronger loving and nurturing relationships

---

33 YEHUIAH
34 LEHAHIAH
35 CHAVAKIAH
36 MENADEL
37 ANIEL
38 HAAMIAH
39 REHAEL
40 YEIAZEL

4/23 * 7/7 * 9/19 * 12/1 * **2/9**

33 YEHUIAH

(vay-HOO-ee-YAH)

Subordination to Higher Order (R)

'One who calls you to higher ground'

Archangel ~ CHAMAEL

Virgo / Uranus (9/3-7)

I AM THAT WHICH...

helps to improve the 'existing order' by bringing the values of heart and soul into your motivations and into worldly constructions that strive to benefit all. It is a deep and holy urge of your nature to create and achieve. In doing so you re-enact the first act of Creation by the Divine Itself, which was born out of Its desire to know what It was and what more It might become through Its creations. Thus, your own worldly creations are all good in and of themselves – but their ultimate value is in your intent and use of them. The question is, do you add to the wholeness of the world through your endeavors and creations, or do you create a hole in the world by taking from it without giving something holy – something loving and true – of yourself in return?

When the bigger picture of soul purpose ennobles your worldly bottom lines, what you value for yourself and your loved ones will also be what you value for your neighbors near and far. At the heart of the bigger picture, the bottom line becomes not about who wins a war but who will stop warring to win the battle that cannot be fought. Here it is not about who wins the race, but who stays in it...not who gets there first, but who uses their advantage to give a leg up to those who come after...not who makes the most money and has the most success, but who makes the most OF money and success so that all may have a chance to thrive.

These things I say may not seem to apply to you as an individual – but understand that all of you contribute to and are affected in one way or another by the conditions in your world – whether through thoughts, feelings, actions or inaction. Thus do I give you my light as YEHUIAH that you may see beyond the contrived bottom lines of your industries and organizations that have sometimes pushed your souls so far down inside you that you do not find them again until you are floundering at the 'bottom of your barrels,' groping for meaning and hope when all else is lost. A loving and true higher order cannot find its way to the outer world unless you each bring it to the world from the Divine within you which you carry in your soul.

You came here to do this – to show the Divine and the Human that the 'stuff' of the eternal can dwell in and even expand time, that meaning can be ensouled in matter, that the values of the Heavens can ennoble the Earth and give a greater life to all who live. The portal to your soul-remembering is your heart. Submit your life, your thoughts, your words and actions to the higher order of your heart – and your heart will lead you deeper in to the sovereignty of your soul and bring it forth into the whole of your life. Then you may know what it is to live and why the gift of life was so lovingly and truly given unto you by your Divine Parent. So may it be. Amen...

4/24 * 7/8 * 9/20 + 21am * 12/2 * **2/10**

34 LEHAHIAH

(lay-HA-hee-YAH)

Obedience (R)

'One who amplifies inner authority'

Archangel ~ CHAMAEL

Virgo / Saturn (9/8-12)

I AM THAT WHICH...

helps you to pursue life-affirming purposes in the world that are in alignment with your higher inner authority and which enable you to form allegiances according to principles you can respect and obey. Obedience is a concept that often conjures uncomfortable feelings. Because it challenges your foundational sense of self-will and freedom to choose, the very utterance of the word can raise the 'hackles' of stubbornness – whether you are two or ninety-two! In your Divine-Human beingness, obedience is one of those things, like everything in life, which has two sides. It can be used to oppress, control and tyrannize – or as a focalizing energy to cultivate depth and creativity, purpose, freedom, enlightenment and good works.

Because of the histories of persecution in your world, you have become very aware of the dangers of political and religious tyrannies and tyrants and the disastrous outcomes of 'blind obedience.' But there is another kind of obedience that is more subtle and much more pervasive – and which can be used for the good of all or the 'good' of only a few.

Obedience to the norm – to what is being done or has 'always' been done or what is expected of you at different stages of life – is a way that traditions are built, families raised, goals realized and group agreements and governments formed, for better or worse.

However, it can also be an opiate that dulls or distorts your deeper personal sense of truth and right purpose – and on a broader scale allows you to condone things in your world that need changing. This kind of obedience can be more insidious because it plays to your need for routine and comfort with as little conflict as possible in your daily life. But it is when you become dulled to your deeper values, and thus ultimately apathetic to the effect individual dullness and 'blind obedience' has on the collective psyche, that you individually and as part of the collective can be manipulated and exploited by those with clear and powerful self-interests.

Thus, my light as LEHAHIAH is within you to draw you back to your own within whenever you get those 'twinges' of conscience or questioning about how things are being done in your outer world. You may ask 'what can one person do?' But one person can be a focal point and a clarion call. And one person can join with another, and then you have two from which anything can be born anew in your world. Let your obedience be not to something fixed or unquestioned, which ultimately brings dullness and deadening – but obey the life flow within you that calls upon you to meet the needs and opportunities of the moment. Let the love that originated and expands the truth and integrity of your isness be what you give your obedience to, and join with others doing the same. For in supporting these higher authorities within each other, together you can re-form the world. Amen...

4/25 * 7/9 * 9/21pm + 22 * 12/3 * **2/11**

35 CHAVAKIAH

(cha-VA-kee-YAH)

Reconciliation (R)

'One who resolves paradox'

Archangel ~ CHAMAEL

Virgo / Jupiter (9/13-17)

I AM THAT WHICH...

helps you to tap into the sameness within and among you in order to resolve disputes and differences in values, opinions or goals, and to find vibrancy and enjoyment in your diversities as natural expressions of the diverse nature of life itself. True life-affirming reconciliation is not about imposing the will of one person, interest or faction upon another or making everyone do or be the same. Nor is it about compromise that leaves some disenfranchised or disengaged. With acknowledgment and respect for the value of each other's different offerings, it is about each of you being able to fulfill your purposes and goals in ways that are complementary to the other and the whole.

You, speaking collectively of humankind, have been warring for millennia over your differences of race, culture, creed, personal styles and preferences – and trying to impose your wills and ways upon each other, to your great detriment. Often the underlying fear that has driven suspicion and disrespect of each other's differences is rooted in your sense of the precariousness of life on Earth. The 'unknown' of your own vulnerability causes you to seek conformity, sameness and certainty – thinking or hoping these will give you a sense of safety. If others think, feel, believe and live as you do, you hope that your own underlying doubts and questions may be quelled or at least quieted by having your sense of reality confirmed and engaged in by everyone around you.

But in truth, you need both sameness and difference to live a vibrant Divine-Human life. Your sameness is on the inside in your hearts and souls – in your desire to love and be loved, to know and become more of who you truly are, and to offer something worthwhile to the world from the love and truth of yourself. What makes life interesting for each and all of you is that there are as many different ways to do these same things as there are all of you doing them!

Thus I offer you my CHAVAKIAH light in the very heart of you to help you realize that the key to reconciliation with others in any and all things is to first reconcile your individual self to what makes you different from others. For your uniqueness is key to the proliferation and fulfillment of your life at every level, even as your sameness of heart is vital to being in unity and at peace with yourself and the world. So may you be. Amen...

4/26 * 7/10 * 9/23 * 12/4 * **2/12**

36 MENADEL

(MEH-na-DEL)

Inner/Outer Work (S)

'One who dances two worlds into one'

Archangel ~ CHAMAEL

Virgo / Mars (9/18-23)

I AM THAT WHICH...

helps you to carry your personal integrity and value-based ethics into your work, organizations and social circles so that what you value for you and your loved ones may be manifested and supported in your communities, nations and the greater world. As many of you realize, there has grown a wider and wider gap between what you value on a personal level and what your world is reflecting back to you. Just as your own inner intentions are not always reflected in your outer actions, when this is multiplied times the many the core integrity of your collective actions is compromised and even ruptured.

You are the inner of your outer world, a seed in the soil and the ultimate yield of humanity. What you sow as an individual is magnified and reaped by the multitude, which ultimately comes full circle to impact you and your loved ones. What kind of seed are you? What are you sowing in the world with your attitudes and demeanor, your work and your way of relating with associates, collaborators and even your competitors? Do you keep your word and honor your commitments and responsibilities? Do you sometimes offer a helping hand, an ear for listening and a shoulder for leaning to your neighbor? Do you regard the hopes and dreams of others as important as your own? Do you understand that you need each other's unique contributions in order to achieve your mutual goals, and that your successes are so much more effective and enjoyable when they are shared?

Your world would be a very different place if everyone were working sustainably at something you personally love to do. Wars and disputes are not just about the clashing of political and religious ideologies or infringed-upon territories. Especially in areas where people are repressed and where conditions are harsh and at basic survival levels, conflict is also about economic and existential poverty of the individuals who populate the armies – human beings whose lives have little means or meaning except to take or protect from others whatever they can in order to feed themselves and their families, and even to strike out in anger because of their miseries. These are the end results of a compounded individual and collective unconsciousness that allows for the thriving of the few at the expense of the many.

Thus is my MENADEL light present within you that you may daily strive to align your personal/inner and collective/ outer values. Due to the nature of group and communal dynamics, it is not easy to do this – but it is possible because of the spiritual resources within you as individuals. Dear ones, bring your hearts to the hurting places in your outer world – not just as political and religious altruism – but with personal caring and a true sense of brother-and-sisterhood with your fellow beings. And also with the Earth itself, which feels and absorbs everything you experience. So be it, dear ones, so be it. Amen...

4/27 * 7/11 * 9/24 * 12/5 * **2/13**

37 ANIEL

(AH-nee-EL)

Breaking the Circle (G)

'One who lifts you out of the circle into the light'

Archangel ~ CHAMAEL

Libra / Sun (9/24-28)

I AM THAT WHICH...

helps you to work together with others to increase awareness, visionary thinking and innovative action, so that unproductive patterns and paradigms may be replaced or rehabilitated. All change for better or worse in your world starts with individual attitudes and actions. Thus change for the better starts with the willingness of you and each of your family members, friends and neighbors to bring the life-affirming values that you cherish into your community and local organizations and governments.

As you say, 'you cannot keep doing the same things and expect different results.' But if you fight ***against*** *the old way, then you will fight* ***about*** *it amongst you. A child who continually tries to play with something that is dangerous will not be long deterred by your resistance or admonishment – but give it something more interesting, and it will abandon its old preoccupation without a fight. That child still lives within you all. Thus, rather than forcing out the old, better to offer more life-affirming and productive solutions that others may feel moved to participate in.*

Sameness and status quo – even that which does not serve you – is the protection of familiarity against the unknown of change, and it easily becomes ingrained in your individual and collective subconscious. But sameness can become an opiate that dulls you into apathy, allowing abuses and exploitation to take hold and proliferate. Although to say, 'be the change you want to see' is in danger of becoming so cliché that it loses its vitality in your consciousness, it is a profound instruction for how to change your world – both personally and on global levels.

Therefore is my ANIEL light within you to help you break the circles and cycles of thought and behavior that do not serve the highest good for yourself and others. Look for inspiration from the arts, literatures, philosophies and your 'thought leaders.' And in your quiet times of rumination – or in co-creative conversations with people of like mind and heart, consider what is working and not working in your life and what you could begin to change.

You do not have to be an iconoclast or a visionary at a world podium – though your world needs these. Where there is awareness and even an intent to change, 'shift happens.' Each small change over time adds up exponentially to a changed life, and ultimately a changed world. Together, let us bring the values you cherish for yourself and your loved ones to your neighbors near and far and your endeavors and creations in the world. And by values we don't necessarily mean dogmas, belief systems or ideologies, but the innermost soul-longings and purposes which you carry in the sameness of your hearts. Amen...

4/28 * 7/12 * 9/25 * 12/6 * **2/14**

38 HAAMIAH

(ha-AH-mee-YAH)

Ritual and Ceremony (G)

'One who enlivens the path with love'

Archangel ~ CHAMAEL

Libra / Venus (9/29-10/3)

I AM THAT WHICH...

helps you to use rituals and ceremonies as ways to amplify spiritual presence and cultivate a sense of unity with your extended family of friends and neighbors near and far, including those whose beliefs and practices differ from yours. However diverse may be the details of humankind's many spiritual paths, at the heart of all life-affirming belief systems is the encouragement to increase the presence of love. Whenever you argue with each other over ideologies and dogmas, you have forgotten that. Love is greater than any creed, ritual or ceremony – or lack thereof – and when you fight over the details of your personal preferences, you have lost sight of the heart in each of you that longs for meaning and true connection. If there were any judgment in the cosmos that is not your own (which there is not), you would not be asked when you 'get to heaven' what religion you followed or what holy book you read – but rather, what was in your heart.

Love has the power to fulfill the laws of man and God and bring together what fear has torn asunder and keeps separate. It is not love that turns family members and neighbors against each other, but fear. It is not love that strikes out against others to protect the 'laws' of God or a particular interpretation of God. If beliefs, rituals and ceremonies are not life-and-love-affirming, then they are denyers of Divine Love and Truth. And when they are used to demand conformity and adherence, then the individuation which is your birthright is thwarted. For only through individual becoming may the diversity of the Divine be expressed on Earth through each and all of your unique choices, creations and ways.

Rather than 'banning' religion in your schools, let your educational systems educate about the rituals and belief systems of all cultures. The cure for suspicion and fear of each other's ways is to learn about them. In doing so you discover the similarities at the heart of your different beliefs and practices – just as you do when you get to know someone of a different culture. It is the sameness within that is your gift of familiarity, comfort and kinship to each other – and your outer differences which inspire you to learn and grow beyond your personal sphere. Just ask the young people who have used your 'social networking' phenomena to meet people of like mind and heart all over the world!

And thus my light as HAAMIAH is given unto you to look into each other's hearts when you cannot understand each other's ways. If you cannot find likeness in your ideologies, meet at the heart. Rather than railing against a whole group or society of people whose ways you disagree with, seek out the heart of one of them with your own and you will find a brother or a sister. Do these things and you will find yourselves as you find each other. Amen...

4/29 * 7/13 * 9/26 * 12/7 * **2/15**

39 REHAEL

(RAY-ha-EL)

Filial Submission (G)

'One who honors what was while inspiring what will be'

Archangel ~ CHAMAEL

Libra / Mercury (10/4-8)

I AM THAT WHICH...

helps you to maintain respectful and mutually vibrant hierarchies in business, politics, society and organizations of all kinds so as to combine positive past practices and achievements with new ideas, visions and innovations. In many of your consumer-driven societies, there is a reverence for innovation with built-in 'obsolescence' in order to ensure a continual audience and drive the urge for the acquisition of things. While this can create exciting and fast-paced economics, it can also diminish respect for quality and longevity, value, the contributions of elders, quality of life, and the wisdom of hard-won lessons and past innovations which support present and future generations and creations.

We would sometimes like to say to you slow down a little! Let the quantity of your creations be wisely tempered by attention to their quality and long-range usefulness and impact. In addition to your focus on how many you can make and sell in as short a time as possible – make your creations better and longer-lasting. Use your creativity to come up with new and inspired creations, rather than endless versions of the same thing with different packaging, 'bells and whistles' or 'delivery systems.' When creativity is forced to be fast-paced, you don't have the inner quiet for truly inspired ideas – so you copy from each other instead of creating something new. The pressure to produce for contrived consumer demands, 'funding protocols' and 'quarterly reports' is often the underlying reason why, for example, your health industries continue to focus on symptom management rather than research for true cures – which requires a more depthful immersion in 'whatever time it takes.'

Your world needs thinkers and creators whose vision encompasses both the past and the future – not just producers who are interested only in short-term gain, again and again. Just as the Earth itself needs the nutrients of contributions from past seasons, so does the human psyche need rootedness in the soil of what came before in order to branch out into the new light of day every day. When you push the river, force the flow or artificially stimulate growth before its natural time, you disturb the natural balance – and every species of being on Earth is deeply and harmfully affected by this in one way or another, sooner or later.

Thus, dear one and ones, use your power individually and collectively, and mine as REHAEL, to respect all of life, and to realize that what you are bringing into being today rests on the shoulders of yesterday and weighs on the shoulders of tomorrow. Bring heart to all you do, so that your soul-memories can gather up both time and the eternal for the greaterness of your makings. Heart: your most creative and visionary resource. 'Don't leave home (or yesterday) without it!' Amen...

4/30 * 7/14 * 9/27 * 12/8 * **2/16**

40 YEIAZEL

(YAY-ah-ZEL)

Divine Consolation and Comfort (G)

'One who is a soft landing for your heart'

Archangel ~ CHAMAEL

Libra / Moon (10/9-13)

I AM THAT WHICH...

helps to support an inspiring atmosphere that draws on the eternal to uplift people and circumstances and to create resonance among hearts in order to bring together those of different minds. In a world with so much diversity of species, language, race, creed, culture and more, only one language speaks to everyone regardless of your differences. And that is, of course, the language of the heart – because therein lies your sameness with each other. Thus, it is not the persuasion of knowledge, ideologies, politics, religions or philosophies that will bring true comfort and generosity of spirit among you. It is the dialects of love – care, kindness, compassion, forgiveness, truth and wisdom – these things which are born in you of the Divine, carried in your souls and communicated to and among your hearts. No matter who you are or what your background, influences or contexts, when someone comes to you with heart, that which is in the deepest part of you feels the tug of recognition and is moved.

One of the most common and important ways that you share resonance of heart is by telling and listening to each other's stories. Who living on your Earth has not loved and dreamed, had longings and disappointments, lost something or someone cherished and felt the depths of pain? Who does not need healing or renewal in some way? It is said in your holy books, 'that which you do for the least among you, you do for me' – and this is because the Divine dwells within and experiences life as each and all of you. Your comfort of each other is a sacred re-enactment of the Divine Love that waits in every heart to be given, shared and received – even unto the creatures that share your home and planet, the Earth itself and every living and growing thing.

Thus does my comforting light as YEIAZEL warm the ways and words between and among you. Thus do I as the caring of the Divine Heart quicken your listening ears, your shoulders for leaning, your embraces of empathy and caring, and especially, your mercy and forgiveness of each other. For you must know this: every being and thing feels. Animals, plants and even that which seems to be inanimate, registers what goes on within and among you. The Earth itself rejoices and sorrows with you. The waters soothe your emotional tides and wash away yesterday. The creatures feel your love and your fear. The trees and flora of all kinds absorb your weary energies, give you air to breathe and invite your eyes and heart skyward to the life-giving light of the sun. All the while teaching you about rootedness, resiliency and the beauty of branching out!

Everywhere are threads of love and light. Pull on those threads in another and feel them ripple between you. You are all woven together in the tapestry of life that the Divine Heart weaved from the Love and Truth of Itself. You are not alone. You are never alone, and you are known and felt utterly. And at times dear ones...remind each other. Amen...

February 17 – 24

Angels 41 – 48

Sephira 6

TIPHARETH ~ Beauty, Harmony

Overlighting Archangel

MIKHAEL ~ 'Who is as God'
(Governs with RAPHAEL*) Power and will; ignites strength, courage and protection for spiritual seeking and healing

---

41 HAHAHEL
42 MIKAEL
43 VEULIAH
44 YELAHIAH
45 SEALIAH
46 ARIEL
47 ASALIAH
48 MIHAEL

* Note that the Archangel correspondences in Sephirot 6 and 8 have been interchanged throughout the centuries by different Kabbalists and schools of thought. After additional research which shows the ways in which both Archangels are active in both Sephirot, the primary Archangel correspondences presented in the original *Birth Angels* book are reversed here, but each are included as co-governing.

5/1 * 7/15 * 9/28 * 12/9 * **2/17**

41 HAHAHEL

(HAH-hah-HEL)

Mission (R)

'One who brings Heaven to Earth'

Archangel ~ MIKHAEL (with RAPHAEL)

Libra / Uranus (10/14-18)

I AM THAT WHICH...

helps you to create or cooperate in endeavors that encourage individual becoming and the greater soul-expression of each and all according to your unique talents, passions and purposes. Your soul mission, in whatever context expressed, takes you on this journey: to love, heal and create...love, heal and create, again and again. In this life-affirming cycle, love gives you access to the eternal, which provides what is needed for healing, which increases your capacity to love and create, which helps you to keep healing. Thus in due time you may blossom and burst forth with the most delicious unique fruit for your own delectable life experience – and so that the Divine within you may be increased, and your fellow beings may be inspired to their own greater becoming.

And you thought you were here to simply make money, provide for yourself and your family, buy whatever you want and pass it on when you leave? Ha! Tip of the iceberg! These are not goals – they are stages for the playing out of your Divine-Human beingness – people and places of belonging and doing that give you human comfort and relatedness while your soul is surreptitiously doing what it really came here to do: ***To grow the love and truth of your own humanity, so that you might share and multiply the Divine on Earth in diverse and meaningful relatings and co-purposing with others.***

It is common to become so compelled by the pleasures or challenges of Earth-life that your innermost desires and longings recede. But in all your dissatisfactions, depressions, 'mid-life crises' and more, it is your forgotten soul that is calling to you. And no amount of self-medication or 'looking for love in all the wrong places' can banish or satisfy this healthy spiritual urge from within you that is the deepest part OF you. Thus, we of the Divine are here in your own within to amplify and help you answer this urge.

Know also that if it is your mission to help others realize theirs, it is more helpful to respect their context of inclination, talents, preferences and potential than to try to convert them to your own ways. Teachers and mentors in every field and industry who see not only who you are now – but what more of yourself you can be – are the inspiring angels among you! Your first teachers are your parents, and then friends, associates, those you admire, and some you don't. In every moment of mentoring – through presence and listening, deliberance or happenstance – you are helping each other to become more of who you truly are. Even when steered in the 'wrong' direction at times, it is temporarily the right one if it helps you to realize where you really want to go!

For all this and more, dear missioning soul, my Angelic light as HAHAHEL is given to reside within you so that when you venture too far into forgetting, my Divine Love-light can be a beacon for return. Amen...

5/2 * 7/16 * 9/29 * 12/10 * **2/18**

42 MIKAEL

(MIH-kah-EL)

Political Authority and Order (R)

'One who helps you find your guiding light'

Archangel ~ MIKHAEL (with RAPHAEL)

Libra / Saturn (10/19-23)

I AM THAT WHICH...

helps to increase the capacity for individual self-governing, mutual care and rehabilitation of systems so that your organizational authorities are more reflective of your highest ideals and life-affirming potential for all. Any politics or philosophy concerning a 'higher world order' must address humanity at the individual level to have any hope of transforming the use of authority in Earth-life. It is one thing to need administrative protocols and governing bodies to help organize the group dynamics of living and working and caring for each other. It is a whole other thing to need police and military to <u>*protect*</u> *yourselves against each other.*

Everything that is 'wrong,' dysfunctional or antagonistic in your societies starts with a hurting, afraid, angry, resentful or disturbed individual, which often inspires similar individuals – which can then multiply into dissident or violent groups, and then policing organizations and armies to counter them, which turn out more individuals that continue the cycle. As so many of you are seeing in nations that rely heavily on curbing violence with more violence, this modality doesn't heal or cure – it only grows the problem. At its 'best,' violence begets an uneasy and temporary peace in which the perceived offenses and resentments that foster violence are suppressed but continue to fester. But there are ways you can start right now to make changes for the better of all by addressing ALL the contributing factors on individual and societal levels, for example: repurpose existing protocols and create laws that curb the accessibility of violent means; help families in local communities to support individual well-being, or lack thereof, and the ability for every person to get what is needed for mental, physical and spiritual health, as well as education and work; and implement programs that help young people to develop a sense of purpose and belonging, and to foster the desire for a loving and meaningful life – especially those who have been marginalized by poverty and lack of opportunity.

Remember that each of you is a seed of potential in time and eternity. Plant yourself in higher ground and 'go forth and multiply' into parents, teachers and leaders who inspire and encourage and are not harsh taskmasters. Appreciate your artists, mystics and visionaries who dare to seek truth and meaning and proliferate the higher ideals of humanity. Learn from colleagues and nations who collaborate rather than compete. Become sisters and brothers who share and learn from your differences without fear or disdain. Be friends and neighbors to each other far and wide who lift each other up so that each may flower in the uniqueness of your Divine-Human beingness. ***It is about creating a world order based more on what you can give than get – and finally realizing that if everyone is giving, everyone will get what they need, and so much more.***

I tell you this as MIKAEL: However impractical and slow these things may seem in coming, as your numbers grow and the Divine Light becomes more and more recognizable in your radiant hearts, it will be easier for more to join in cooperative being and belonging. And though the 'haters' may resist at first because of their own fears and hurts, eventually they too will come around because there is not one among you who does not want to be loved and to live in a more loving world. This is the 'new world order' to aspire to – one in which love, caring and trust is readily available, so that one by one, person and nation, you may live by inner authorities that are shared by all. Amen...

5/3 * 7/17 * 9/30 * 12/11 * **2/19**

43 VEULIAH

(vay-OO-lee-AH)

Prosperity (R)

'One who shines the light of possibility'

Archangel ~ MIKHAEL (with RAPHAEL)

Scorpio / Jupiter (10/24-28)

I AM THAT WHICH...

helps you to interact with your world with love, compassion and kindness in order to enter the flow of infinite possibility and create the feelings and experience of prosperity for yourself and others. When material assets become over-valued, it is easy for your everyday orientation to become about acquisition and short-term gain. To those who have less means to 'keep up' with the pace of immediate gratification, abundance can seem elusive, exclusive and short-lived. True prosperity is less about the quantity of what you own, and more about the quality of your life and relationship with people and things that enrich your life through feeling, being and doing.

There are two ways that prosperity is created in your world: by giving or taking. In both scenarios you can get what you need or want, but there are important differences between them. Giving, and the receiving which completes it, create infinite potential, whereas taking has an expiration date. Through giving you and the receiver both receive a sense of prosperity that self-regenerates. Because of the inherent love-energy of giving, something more will be created of it by and in the person who receives it – and also in the giver. With taking you get pretty much only the thing you take, which sooner or later will run out. Taking thus diminishes the value of the thing taken, the person or place it was taken from, and the person who took it!

Know that the Divine Itself and all the natural laws of the universe desire that you proliferate and increase. Indeed, the nature of the universe is cosmically hard-wired, so to speak, for expansion. And that which brings expansion with the most potential to keep growing is ***love****, because* ***love is the creation energy of the cosmos and all of life****. Love will expand, multiply and increase what is presented to it. But here's the catch – love expands only true and life-affirming energies. As to anything else, if you allow it, love will first set about transforming it to something life-affirming so that love CAN expand it. That said, there are other energies which create expansion such as greed and the desire for power – especially if you 'love' these ways of being! The resulting abundance, however, will be finite and tainted, and there will always be the need to protect it lest someone or something try to take it from you. Only love can draw from and expand the infinite – and for whatever may be lost in the tides of life, the flow of love will replace in one way or another.*

Thus, I offer you my light as VEULIAH to help you cultivate the creation dynamic of love in your personal life and purpose so that you might more comfortably 'take it on the road' in your worldly endeavors and interactions. Nothing is more love-and-life-affirming than the truth of who you are. Thus, to seek and find the truth of yourself – your unique isness – you must be prepared to love because indeed, you will not know the whole truth of yourself or be able to grow your truth without love. Love what you do as an expansion of your truth, and you will inspire others to do the same. Let love be a wellspring inside you, and you will create more satiating love wherever you go. Be love, and you will always be prosperous, in one way or another, in time and eternity. Amen.

5/4 * 7/18 * 10/1 * 12/12 * **2/20**

44 YELAHIAH

(yay-LA-hee-YAH)

Karmic Warrior (R)

'One who heals the past by loving it.'

Archangel ~ MIKHAEL (with RAPHAEL)

Scorpio / Mars (10/29-11/2)

I AM THAT WHICH...

helps you to participate in healing the accumulation of pain, inhumanity and dissociation of meaning and values in your organizations and communities. All of you come to Earth because of your soul's urge to experience its Divine potential amidst all the wonders and challenges of human life. This includes loving, healing, feeling, doing and learning specific things that can only be experienced on Earth in physicality and relationship – and thereby to be of service to your fellow beings. Your soul, as a unique spark of the Divine, chooses life as the urge of the Divine Itself to experience life through your particular constellation of Divine-Human beingness. The well-being of the 'soul of the world' and the soul of your endeavors, organizations, communities and nations needs you to bring the values and meaning that you personally cherish into your worldly means and machinations.

As old as creation itself are the cosmic laws of attraction and resonance which govern 'whatsoever you sow, that shall you reap.' You understand this as 'what goes around comes around.' But it is not that you are being punished in the coming around for what you once did – rather it is life's way of balancing itself energetically. Thus when one harmful act begets another harmful act (as the work of 'like attracting like'), this can awaken awareness, create a shift in consciousness and bring the willingness to heal and change.

To be a 'karmic warrior' is to realize and take responsibility for the fact that both your hurt and your healing radiate out to all other beings energetically like ripples from a stone thrown into a pond. Ultimately the ripples turn into waves of collective consciousness that shape your world. Waves of hate, dissension and distorted ideologies can crash on the shores of your hearts like tsunamis of unbridled pain. But it is ***love*** *that creates the grandest waves of all, with the power to travel the farthest – even unto the heavens – as they amass the collective empathy, compassion and unity to purify and heal all in their path.*

So dear one and all, use my YELAHIAH light within you to see the ancestral 'dominoes' of cause and effect behind every difficult and destructive event. Do not be looking for blame or revenge, but an understanding of all contributing factors so that you will know how and what to heal – and that all are called to participate in the healing. Let us help you to heal your personal pain lest it become everyone's pain. Let us help you to feel your own worth so that you can feel the value of all. Let us help you to open your hearts so that you might see the sameness under each other's differences. Let us help you find the meaning your humanity seeks in the life-affirming purposes of your Divine souls. And may you find peace and joy for the time you are on Earth that you may bring these to the world that needs what only you can give in your unique way and wonder. Amen...

5/5 * 7/19 * 10/2 * 12/13 * **2/21**

45 SEALIAH

(say-A-Lee-YAH)

Motivation and Willfulness (S)

'One who fires your heart-motor'

Archangel ~ MIKHAEL (with RAPHAEL)

Scorpio / Sun (11/3-7)

I AM THAT WHICH...

helps to motivate you with enthusiasm and a sense of choice during periods of seeming dormancy so that new ideas and ways of being can begin to germinate with vibrancy and strength. In all your seasons of living and creating, there are times when growth is hidden, perhaps just below your consciousness. Gardeners understand this well, trusting that time, light, warmth and nutrient-rich soil will bring new life to the surface in due time. The time when growth is not visible is often when the greatest amount of growth is occurring. This is when a seeming nothing is becoming something in the soil of thought, feeling and imagination – just as when the embryo of a living being is developing its physical form inside the womb. Maintaining motivation and enthusiasm while formation is taking the time it takes is one of the keys to ultimate success. So whether you are growing yourself, raising children, creating a new project, organization or community initiative, trust the process. Be willing to attune, listen and keep the nutritive flow of love and awareness vibrant with a sense of purpose and right motivation.

A lack of will for doing something or 'going the distance' with it is usually an indication that motivation is lacking. One must truly want something in order to be motivated. In addition, if there are underlying doubts about the truth or rightness of an endeavor, or a sense of undeserving or inability, the will to do it will likely be lukewarm at best. And stubbornness is a poor substitute for a rightly motivated will – like your saying about the dog who doesn't want the bone, but doesn't want anyone else to have it either! When this gets magnified beyond the individual level, motivations become corrupted with 'special interests' and 'hidden agendas' of groups, corporations, nations and their leadership. Ultimately, the sovereignty of will for all people degrades into a stifling aggression, on the one hand, and apathy on the other – both void of true caring for fellow beings.

Thus is my SEALIAH light given to dwell within you, to help keep your motivations noble and your will unencumbered and strong, especially while you and your ideas are still germinating. Why you do what you do – and the strength, determination and courage with which you do it – is just as important to the greater world as it is in your personal realm and relatings. Every thought, feeling, intent and action is registered in the collective consciousness of not only your own humankind, but in all living beings and things, including the Earth itself. In the simplest terms, it's about being motivated by what is life-affirming for all. Heart-motivated, heart-centric living. Because it is true and right and loving. Because it will bring you infinite joy. Amen...

5/6 * 7/20 * 10/3 * 12/14 * **2/22**

46 ARIEL

(AH-ree-EL)

Perceiver and Revealer (G)

'One who demystifies the mysteries'

Archangel ~ MIKHAEL (with RAPHAEL)

Scorpio / Venus (11/8-12)

I AM THAT WHICH...

helps you to cultivate inner seeing of the Divine mysteries at play within humanity: how the eternal seeds time, how the Divine seeds the individual, and how the individual seeds all of humanity and the collective consciousness. In order to truly see the ever-present 'more than meets the eye' about anyone and any thing or circumstance in your world, you must be able to see the whole within the part, the part within the whole, and which part of the whole each part expresses! Inner seeing uses the 'bigger picture' vision of the eternal and can help you to discern the underlying dynamics of relatedness among you and all beings and things which move you forward in time individually and together. In developing self-perception, you come to know who you are to and for yourself, the value you bring to your community and world, and how you and your world affect and effect each other. In this, and also in helping others to develop more clarity of self-perception, you must look not just with your eyes and your mind, but your heart and soul – which can see the fluid and ever-evolving truth of each and all.

The eyes often see only what is apparent, based on what is wanted or needed to be seen. And the mind sees mostly what it has seen before and categorized into something it can recognize again. Heart-and-soul seeing sees not only what is right in front of you or another, but also what is over there, beyond or underlying, still on its way into the time and place of the present. Heart-and-soul seeing uses the 'all-access pass' of eternal love and truth to see greater meaning and purpose under visible presentations and patterns – like the as yet unsprouted light-seeds within people which hold the soul-print for who they long to be. Likewise, in mining for greater truths in your societies, when you look through the eyes of love you can see how individuals have seeded the behaviors and thinking trends of the masses – and how, by coming together as unified individuals, you can create change.

Love and truth are always seeking the equilibrium that occurs when polarities realize that they do not oppose, but rather complement, complete and catalyze each other through their cycles of change and growth. Always know that any truth you seek or find is not a whole truth unless you are looking through the eyes of love. And that when you choose to reveal the truths you see, others will be better able to recognize and receive them if they are accompanied by love, in search of equilibrium and harmony.

And so, dear seer-sayer, draw upon my love-and-truth light as ARIEL within you, the better to see and say truth in a way that inspires more of the same. Remember that any proffered truth that causes blame, shame or division is only a part-truth – and one that will likely cause resentment and resistance. For no matter what truths you reveal to others, what truly wants to be seen, heard and felt is the possibility for love and peace. So may it be. Amen...

5/7 * 7/21 * 10/4 * 12/15 * **2/23**

47 ASALIAH

(ah-SA-lee-YAH)

Contemplation (G)

'One who sees the patterns and purposes'

Archangel ~ MIKHAEL (with RAPHAEL)

Scorpio / Mercury (11/13-17)

I AM THAT WHICH...

helps to make your life a template for what you want the world to be, and to work in awareness with others toward a shift in collective consciousness for cooperative and compassionate living. All outer states of being and doing for you as an individual begin in the inner realms of thought, feeling, creativity, intention and willingness. These compose your inner template for outer manifestation. Thus, who you each are as individuals determines the quality of your communities and organizations. And just as your individual states of being are causal to the states of being in your collectives, your collective envisionings and dynamics seed the whole world. You are all lamps and light-bearers. The challenge is to not invest, identify with or engage in negative events – or even fight them – but to hold a template within your heart for what you want to see materialize so that your awareness and attention become a light-magnet for intention and fulfillment.

Many of your organizations and communities fester with the contagion of negative attitudes and fears that one or more individuals have initiated. But all it takes is one person with heart-wisdom and positive conviction to begin to turn the tide toward awareness and compel the hearts of others with what is true and right. That person sometimes needs to be you, but you do not stand alone in that light. Though it may feel so with your first word or step, your affirmative intention is instantly broadcast from here to the heavens – and by your second step we are right here with and among you, moving the hearts, hands and feet of others to join you!

One of the gifts in your togetherness is that you may remind each other of the vision you hold for higher being and doing among you. Support those in your communities and societies who carry artistic and philosophical 'banners' for your highest ideals, and do not mock them for naiveté, impracticality or imperfection. It is not an easy life to be a light in the darkness for others, especially if that light is living with its own shadows. You are each called to the world because of your uniqueness – not your perfection.

And so I say to you as ASALIAH, do what only you can do to change the world by fashioning your own life as a template for the kind of world you want to live in. What this means essentially, every day and moment, is to "do unto others what you would have them do unto you" – rather that just what they do to you. And realize that no one can do anything to you unless on some level you are letting them. Let this be the template for your valuing of self and your interactions with all. At the same time, accept where you are at any given moment while keeping what you aspire to be as a 'star in the sky of your heart.' Follow where it leads, and when your earthly concerns pull you elsewhere, let that eternal heart-light bring you back. And no matter what anyone says or does, don't believe anything but love. Amen...

5/8 * 7/22 * 10/5 * 12/16 * **2/24**

48 MIHAEL

(MIH-a-EL)

Fertility and Fruitfulness (G)

'One who taps the light-elixirs of life'

Archangel ~ MIKHAEL (with RAPHAEL)

Scorpio / Moon (11/18-22)

I AM THAT WHICH...

helps you to fertilize collaborations and partnerships with energies, ideas, personnel and resources needed to bring fruition to endeavors and enterprises in ways that are life-affirming for all. When you are creating on your own, your collaborators are often the inner 'muses' that inspire and guide your creative process. In attunement with what is being created, you can feel the energy and momentum that nurtures the developing form as it draws on your passions, talents and skills to come into full fruition. When you collaborate with 'visible others' you are not only listening to your own within, but also to the inspirations and ideas of your co-creators. As your collective creativities are combined, your creation cup will runneth over with the magic of 'quantum multiplicity' that happens where two or more are gathered in common intent, mutual encouragement and an enthusiastic exchange of ideas!

Something that must be balanced in collaborations is the natural urge of individuation and the desire to be recognized for your own contributions. This reflects the often uneasy dance between individuality and unity in your life as a human being. Each of you are seeking to cultivate and express your own true being and purpose – and indeed that is vital in what you are here to do. You will come to realize, however, that the more you are able to be and express the love and truth of yourself, the more you will have to contribute in creating something in togetherness that is bigger than any one of you – which can only materialize because of ALL of you.

I tell you as MIHAEL that despite any seeming limitations in your world, your inner fertility is not bound or limited by time and place. Thus dear infinitely fertile ones, draw forth as much of my creation-light as your hearts can hold between and among you to amplify your creations. And importantly, allow the space of time your creations need to gestate and form their foundational aspects, for this is when they are tapping the timelessness that cultivates depth and meaning. If there should occur a barrenness in the yield of your endeavors, look to the soil in which they were seeded. Enthusiasm, willingness and cooperation draw forth inspiration, innovation and manifestation; whereas half-heartedness, fear, protectiveness and jealousy cause aridity, blockage and stagnation.

Whatsoever you create, draw on the energies of the inner Divine that dwell within your heart and soul, so that what emerges will bring with it the universalities of love and truth that 'hit home' in very personal ways within others. And know that the sweetest fruit of any bounty is that which disseminates unto your fellow beings the seeds of mutual compassion, respect and an ever-deepening capacity for loving. Amen...

February 25 – March 4

Angels 49 – 56

Sephira 7

NETZACH ~ Victory

Overlighting Archangel

HANIEL ~ 'Grace of God'
Joy, light, insight and true unselfish love through relationship with the Divine

---

49 VEHUEL
50 DANIEL
51 HAHASIAH
52 IMAMIAH
53 NANAEL
54 NITHAEL
55 MEBAHIAH
56 POYEL

5/9 * 7/23 * 10/6 * 12/17 * **2/25**

49 VEHUEL

(VAY-hoo-EL)

Elevation, Grandeur (R)

'One who in-spirits the magnificence of the higher'

Archangel ~ HANIEL

Sagittarius / Uranus (11/23-27)

I AM THAT WHICH...

helps to heighten your awareness to the greater significance in the daily and the mundane, as well as in important and difficult events, and that by ennobling your own life you may help to ennoble the world. As an individual seed of humanity, whatever you bring forth to the world starts with your own thoughts, feelings, attitudes, actions and state of being. Thus, if you want a better world, the place to start is always with yourself. Your personal outlook determines how you look out at the world and what you notice, which will increase more of the same. If you look for the higher ground within yourself, then you will look for, see and contribute to higher ground 'out there.' If you don't succumb to the 'lowest common denominator' of thought or feeling in yourself, but play to your own higher potential – you will more easily do so with everyone and everything else. Elevating your experiences and encounters is essentially about raising the vibration of yourself as an individual and carrying that into group consciousness. You can most easily do that if you let both your heart and mind play their parts in exercising compassion, awareness and perspective over judgment, ignorance and 'mono-vision.'

Here are just a few examples of how elevating your perception can help you to change your experience and enable you to 'better' perceive and interact with the larger world:

** See personal 'bad' news and events as symptoms of where healing is needed = perceiving global events in the same way and focusing on mutual responsibility for healing rather than blame.*

** Regard a seeming setback in your personal or public life as a chance to reconsider goals or methods, focus inner and outer resources, and start again = being open to change and willing to rehabilitate and repurpose community energies and actions.*

** Use not getting what you want when you want it as an opportunity to appreciate what you have, while coming up with a different way to get the feeling you think it will give you in having it = curbing the need to constantly acquire and consume, and buying or helping to create products with more quality and longevity.*

** Change a grumpy attitude by smiling and* ***acting as if*** *you're not (a few smiles in, and you won't be!) = you'll improve the mood and day of everyone you meet!*

Dear ascending one, use my VEHUEL light to shine on, even if you have to do it in the dark! You do not need to have 'perfected' yourself in order to contribute positively to the world. In fact, it is in the world – through relationship of all kinds – where you put into practice what you learn theoretically within yourself. The bottom line is how you bring your authentic heart and higher mind to the world of others – because whenever you do that, the world is better and nobler for it. Amen...

5/10 * 7/24 * 10/7 * 12/18 * **2/26**

50 DANIEL

(DAH-nee-EL)

Eloquence (R)

'One who uses words to bring forth life'

Archangel ~ HANIEL

Sagittarius / Saturn (11/28-12/2)

I AM THAT WHICH...

helps you to be authentic, true and relatable in speech and communication of all kinds so that you may instill trust, respect and friendship while also inspiring higher ideals and potentials. Communication is vital to your quality of relating at every level of life. The first words you say to someone constitute your last chance to make a welcoming first impression! Many throw out words carelessly, not realizing how powerful they are. You cannot, as you say, 'unring the bell' of disrespectful or insensitive words resounding in another person's heart and mind. From the beginning of Creation, words have become 'flesh.' Like everything else in the duality of Earth-life, words, images and other forms of communication have enormous power to create or destroy. The use of these powers are in the realm of your free will – and it is your birthright to choose how to express yourself. But your rights also involve responsibility, for everything you do and say has an energetic impact upon others – including those who are far beyond your immediate vicinity. As with all rights, ***just because you can doesn't mean you always should.***

'The lines get blurred,' as you say, from when communication crosses the line from being a social or moral challenge and an instrument of truth-seeking – to when it becomes a weapon of mockery and disdain. 'Freedom of speech' can degrade into

bullying, shaming, disrespect or a catalyst of violence to self or others. Self-expression can become lost in self-importance. If the pen is to be 'mightier than the sword,' then the pen must do what the sword cannot. If words are to be more than pointers to meaning, then they must have the heart to heal...to inspire compassion and possibility...enable understanding and cooperation...even bring forth new life.

Your whole lifetime is a moment at the podium of both time and eternity. What message would you like to be broadcasting? What feelings and wisdoms would you like to seed in the hearts and minds of others? What words of being and doing would you like to contribute to the multi-verse poem of Creation? Dear one, as the light of DANIEL I can see how greatly your soul desires to use its own Divine-Human potential to inspire and be of beneficent service to others!

There are many languages spoken in your world, and many ways to understand and misunderstand each other. But the language that is never misunderstood, no matter what dialect it is spoken in, is the language of the heart. When the heart speaks, compassion speaks...wisdom speaks...a whole truth speaks that can only be known in the presence of love. Thus, dear one if you would speak words that anyone in the world might understand, let them be spoken by that part of you which your own soul trusts with its message and purpose – the beautiful life-affirming treasure of your heart. Amen...

5/11 * 7/25 + 26am * 10/8 * 12/19 * **2/27**

51 HAHASIAH

(ha-HAH-see-YAH)

Universal Medicine (R)

'One who draws from the Oneness to heal'

Archangel ~ HANIEL

Sagittarius / Jupiter (12/3-7)

I AM THAT WHICH...

helps to reawaken the soul-memory of Oneness in order to heal any sense of unbelonging, aloneness and fear for self so that separatism, greed and the need for power can begin to be transformed in your world. At the root of so many of your societal ills are the mistaken notions that you are 'born alone and die alone,' and thus it's 'every man for himself' in a 'dog-eat-dog world' where 'survival of the fittest' (richest-prettiest-biggest-baddest-loudest) rules, and 'the best man always wins.'

The thing is, you're not alone. Never were, never are, never will be! *When you fall down the rabbit hole of your own fear, you forget that the great 'cosmic banker' and its deal-of-a-lifetime unlimited credit line of eternal and unconditional love* ***always*** *has your back! You forget because only your heart knows that (thanks to your soul which uses your heart as its broadcaster). But when you're consumed with fear, you're not thinking or feeling with your heart, since fear has displaced all the inner awareness space wherein love and a comforting sense of otherness resides. Fear tells you there's a limited amount of resources, and that to get something for yourself you may have to take it from someone else – and if you get it, then you have to keep anyone else from taking it. But truly – it's no more fun to be thriving by yourself than to not be thriving by yourself (seemingly 'by yourself').*

No matter how alone or separate you may feel at times, there's always someone 'at home' within. It's just that the fear of your own within possibly being the loneliest and scariest place in the world can keep you from going there. But when you do, this is what you will find...

My divinely medicinal love-light as HAHASIAH resides within you, along with all the Angelic aspects that reflect the beautiful diverse hues of the Divine Itself which power your 'hue-manity!' And we are here, as the collective One with and within you, to heal your hurts, reveal your inherent worth and help you fulfill the love and truth of your unique soul purpose which your fellow beings are waiting for, even needing, you to manifest. And to address any confusions or guilt about how to feel a sense of unity when you're also trying to do what's best for yourself, we say again...

You are here to individuate – to become truly who you are – because in doing so you become a gift and inspiration to the world and a gift to the Divine who experiences life through you as only you can live it. You will see that ***the more you become and increase who you are, the more you will want to give of yourself to others****. And so along the way, just know that while your outer self is doing its thing in the world, your heart can still carry all of humanity within it. And it is your heart which knows that* ***for all that ever ails you or anyone, the active ingredient in any oneness-remedy is love****. Amen...*

5/12 * 7/26pm + 27 * 10/9 * 12/20 * **2/28 + 29**

52 IMAMIAH

(ee-MAH-mee-YAH)

Expiation of Errors (R)

'One who makes whole'

Archangel ~ HANIEL

Sagittarius / Mars (12/8-12)

I AM THAT WHICH...

helps to instill a sense of collective responsibility for correcting the societal issues which cause rampant disruptions of peace, trust and well-being within your communities and world. Many in your world are despairing of how things will ever change for the better. So many peoples and nations still live under tyrannical and terrorizing rule – and even those who live with the rights and freedoms that others are being deprived of are themselves being tyrannized by the fruits of their own sowing and reaping and those among them who have been marginalized by poverty and bias. Ultimately, however, real change comes not by fighting the error, but implementing life-affirming solutions that are more attractive and compelling than the destructive compulsions of error. Sooner or later, you must address the cause, not only the effect, in order to bring about a cure. Both cause and cure are multi-faceted, and will need the 'response-ability' of you and all, even for that which was precipitated generations ago.

At the root of much of your crime, violence and terror across the world are these things: (1) fear, suspicion, ignorance and intolerance of each other's diversities of race, culture, creed and gender; (2) greed, excessive profiteering and power-mongering which takes from many to give to the few; (3) disenfranchisement and marginalization of certain peoples which results in lack of education, means and opportunity suffered by individuals and groups in a world where others seem to have so much more – often because of what was once taken from them; (4) distortions of the natural urge for meaning and purpose, causing someone who feels worthless and outcast to seek any cause or group that offers a sense of purpose, power and belonging, which may also give an outlet for pent-up anger and resentment; (5) exploitation of the disenfranchised by those whose thirst for power and importance take from others their personal sovereignty of heart and mind and leave them with less than nothing, so that they become totally dependent on their exploiters; and (6) dissociation and apathy on the part of those who do not understand, accept or want to engage in collective responsibility – or even self-responsibility.

Those in your world who are creating public conversation about these issues are realizing in examining your local and global histories that individuals or groups of people who have been chronically marginalized – whether by being deprived of their homeland, their basic human rights, education, work or any sense of equality, belonging or worthiness – are often the very people who become society's economic and social burdens, predators and even terrorists. But endlessly blaming, punishing and fighting each other is not the cure. An 'eye for an eye' does not expiate a perceived wrong, but rather ends up just bringing about the blindness of all. Thus the cure is not revenge – or even punishment – but transformation.

You must understand, with compassion, that although all are "created equal," you do not come into this world with equal circumstances, or with an equal ability to withstand the challenges and hardships you may encounter – even though on a soul level you have chosen them. In these cases, often such choices were made in order to bring awareness and help others to develop compassion and kindness. Every person's role has the potential to increase awareness and love where there is willingness and an ability to see the greater reality beyond 'the facts.'

My light as IMAMIAH is given to show you that true expiation involves both correction and atonement which has transformation as its goal. When we say atonement, we mean it in the sense of at-onement – the restoration of unity. It is not blame you are asked to acknowledge, but responsibility for yourself, humanity and the impact you all have on all beings and things, including the natural world. It does not matter whether the fault was on the part of either 'the chicken or the egg.' What matters is that the chicken and the egg are in it together, and both of them need each other. You must stop dancing jerkedly to the 'only human' soundtrack perpetuated by those who think that being marginalized, disempowered, depressed, entitled or exploitive is just 'part of human life.' You are Divine-Human beings, every single one of you. Individually and collectively your soul-mission is to bring Heaven to Earth in ways that only each and all of you can. The petty powers and advantages that so many scramble to acquire are nothing compared to the greater powers of your inner Divine to magnify your individual human experience in glorious heart-and-soul-powered ways that help to magnify all.

Thus dear ones, fill your thinking caps with your feeling hearts and be guided by love, compassion and wisdom to solutions that strive for true caring, concern and well-being for all. What can one person do? – Each of you has a talent, a gift, a message or a skill to contribute. If each and every person attended to the well-being of him or herself and one family member, or one other person in the community – that would accomplish the healing and upliftment of the whole world. It may be hard to conceive, or even do, but it's not impossible! 'Let it come through your hands...' – 'All you need is love...' – "Imagine all the people...' – 'What a world it would be...'

And so be it dear ones, so be it! Amen...

5/13 * 7/28 * 10/10 * 12/21 * **3/1**

53 NANAEL

(NA-na-EL)

Spiritual Communication (R)

'One who sends and receives from within'

Archangel ~ HANIEL

Sagittarius / Sun (12/13-16)

I AM THAT WHICH...

helps you to invoke, inspire and share energies, ideas, knowledge and wisdoms that quicken spiritual awareness and presence among you. Any depthful communication – whether through spoken or written words, imagery, energy or feeling – calls up the inner heart-and-soul-realms of love, truth, meaning and purpose. In this quality of relating, the inner divinity within each of you is stirred. The 'more than meets the eye' of things, people and the mysteries of life becomes apparent, as what is underlying rises to meet your inquiry and exploration. Words transform from pointers to meaning to transmitters of it. Conversation dives beneath the surface and becomes a sounding and catalyst for truth, co-creativity, awareness and change. The present draws from the eternal, and the mutual desire to know quickens the ancient wisdoms between and among vibrant hearts and minds.

Many paths and traditions practiced by humankind have their dedicated vocabularies in which particular words are used as touchstones, triggers and ways to convey beliefs and dogma and inspire spiritual feeling. However, you do not need a religious or spiritual vocabulary to communicate spiritually with each other. As those who have ministered to people of different cultures, creeds and languages have experienced, what is essential can be conveyed by the heart, and often does not even need a verbal language.

Through the universal languages of love, compassion, forgiveness and kindness, you may convey worlds of meaning through feeling. For the affiliated or unaffiliated "everyman-woman," this can be so much more immediate and powerful than having to assimilate a toolbox of vocabulary derived from a particular path or tradition. By 'in-spiriting' the Divine through your own presence, with or without the help of words, imagery or music, you are able to convey the eternal creation energies of love which have the power to inspire new life in heart and mind, as well as body. Through your own fullness of presence and feeling, you embody and enliven Divine Truth and give root to Divine Love within you. From this way of being, you are able to transmit the 'other-worlds' of Spirit into your own and unto the hearts and minds of others – whatever language they speak!

And so I say unto you with my NANAEL light, as you come together with others and allow love to branch out among you from one heart to another, you bring all that is good and God to prevail upon Earth. Therefore do we rejoice for the greaterness of all that you may give, receive and experience. By allowing the Divine within you to amplify your human experience with spiritual presence and power, you are able to fulfill your deepest and noblest desires individually and together, in communion with what is essential for life, love and the truth of who you are. Amen...

5/14 * 7/29 * 10/11 * 12/22 * **3/2**

54 NITHAEL

(NIT-ha-EL)

Rejuvenation and Eternal Youth (S)

'One who grows the rose of foreverness within'

Archangel ~ HANIEL

Sagittarius / Venus (12/17-21)

I AM THAT WHICH...

helps to enliven you and your endeavors with people of diverse qualities and life experiences who bring enthusiasm, new ideas and values that complement and challenge your own and inspire all of you to new heights of imagination, creativity and cooperation. The very things you are often most afraid of are ultimately those which most invigorate you when you dare to approach and engage. When you are learning new things, visiting new places or relating openly and interestedly with people who seem to be very different from you – we feel your renewed vibrancy and even a greater love for life itself. We see also how enlivened you can be when you associate not only with your peers in age and station of life, but also when you mingle with and befriend those who are much younger and older than you – those who are just starting out with their dreams, and those who are reaping the rewards of wisdom from dreams won and perhaps even 'lost.' Many feel that people much younger, older or different are irrelevant to their lives, but nothing could be less true. It is variety and diversity that enriches your life in unexpected and sometimes magical ways.

And so dear body-and-soul vibrancy seeker, I bring you my NITHAEL light – the better for you to see, touch, feel, taste and embrace life at any age in any moment, whether expected or serendipitous. However comfortable and comforting it may be to remain in familiarity and sameness, let not your life or joy be governed by preconceptions, assumptions, normalcy, routine or conformity. Never think you know everything there is to know about anything or anyone, no matter how long you have lived in their proximity. Make it a point to ask a new question every day of your partner, family member or anyone you think you know – or someone you stereotypically think you know who you don't know at all. Make it a probing question that calls for more than a monosyllabic response – and listen to the answer. Not only will you feel rejuvenated by engaging beneath the surface, but so will the other. And if it leads to heartful and co-creative conversation that spawns new ideas or realizations, even better! The heart has access to the eternal by opening to the soul. When you are truly present with someone, you can stop the tick-tock of time together – and there is nothing you cannot imagine, or come to know or be in those clockless moments. Amen...

5/15 * 7/30 * 10/12 * 12/23 * **3/3**

55 MEBAHIAH

(may-BA-hee-YAH)

Intellectual Lucidity (G)

'One who feeds clarity from inner and outer streams'

Archangel ~ HANIEL

Capricorn / Mercury (12/22-26)

I AM THAT WHICH...

helps to cultivate clear thinking and the awareness to discern potential impact of actions and the need for course-correction and change. As many of you feel, a paradigm change much needed in your world is the idea that 'the end justifies the means.' How a thing is done is just as important as what and why, if there is to be true integrity in the final outcome. Your life, your character and your creations are formed more by how you travel the journey than whether you always get to your destination. Lies do not achieve truth, force does not produce freedom, violence does not beget peace. It is difficult to maintain clarity of perspective if decisions are colored by partiality or bias in favor of a particular outcome at any cost. True clarity sees the bigger picture of causes and effects – and especially the long-term impact of not just an end achieved, but what is created or destroyed in the process. Whatever you must do because of work or duty, the soul does not easily bear having to deprive or hurt anyone for even a 'noble cause.'

A clear mind is not possible without the clear-functioning of your other faculties. There is no greater clarity than how the eyes of the wise-heart see. But sometimes you may feel the need to suppress your seeing of the outer world because what is there to see is painful to your personal values – especially if you feel that you don't have the power to change it. But you have so much more power than you know just through your awareness – even to realize that what you are seeing may not be truth, but just the 'tip of the iceberg.' Since often the truth is a submerged mountain of accumulated causes and effects, you must search for truth in a different way. And that way is through the intuition, insight and wisdom that your heart brings to any seeing of person or circumstance.

And so dear one, draw from my MEBAHIAH light to become more and more aware of what is happening around you and in your world. For it is the power of awareness, along with your desire to see something more loving and whole, that starts the energetic ripple of possibility for shift to happen. Many of you hold shame about seeing without committing to action for change. But no, no! – even just your seeing is powerful – especially when you see with love and mercy, rather than judgment of yourself or others.

With clarity of heart and mind, dear one, you can see that all seeming 'evils' happening in your world are accumulated hurts coming to the surface to show where healing is needed. Hold space within your heart for the healing of your world, and take that healing awareness into your day through the way you do what you do and the kindness and willingness you show to family, friends and colleagues. Changing the world can be that simple, and that profound. Amen...

5/16 * 7/31 * 10/13 * 12/24 * **3/4**

56 POYEL

(poi-EL)

Fortune and Support (G)

'One who taps plenitude with feeling'

Archangel ~ HANIEL

Capricorn / Moon (12/27-31)

I AM THAT WHICH...

helps you to harness the spiritual flow of unlimited abundance through the power of positive resonance and the love-in-action that can help to implement systems and solutions for the tangible support and well-being of all. There is infinite abundance in the universe. If you accept that premise, then you must realize that 'there is enough to go around.' But of course, your world doesn't reflect that. When you consider how many people go without even sufficient basic needs, there is obviously a gap between the cosmic bigger picture of infinite flow and humanity's renderings of lack – both on individual and societal levels.

Lack is an attitude, a belief, or a symptomatic circumstance that reflects choosing certain things over others. But lack is not a truth. It may be used by the soul, even whole groups of souls, as a context to challenge creativity and faith in the face of seeming limitation – but lack is not real, although it feels very real to those who experience it. The difficulty in transforming lack is that it is very persuasive. Once you begin to believe in it, it increases. Therefore, the beginning of the cure is to believe not in the illusion you see, but the greater reality that you know is there in your heart and in your universe, waiting and wanting to materialize. Then all you need is to cultivate positive emotion and action as an attraction point and 'quickener' for manifestation!

The same holds true for working to help others manifest what they need and desire. Hold a vision in your own heart and mind for the greater reality of their inherent abundance, and mirror that with positive vibrations, words and actions. Your encouragement and support will stimulate their self-confidence, enthusiasm and creativity and help them to focus on what they can create rather than what they lack! Just with this shift, they can begin to tap their inner and outer resources and turn the tide of their circumstances. This dynamic has occurred in many global communities where entrepreneurs and visionaries have recognized the creative talents of local populations and have set up systems of training and commerce for their development and economic thriving.

The greatest gift for those and any who have been suffering with circumstances of lack is the dignity of having someone believe in their greater possibilities. If you have ever needed this kind of support in your own life, you know that when someone believes in you, you learn to believe in yourself. And that is when everything begins to change.

Thus, dear one, I invite you to draw from my POYEL light to tap the energies of abundance in all you do, and especially to share these energies with those experiencing lack so that they might awaken to the realization of their inner riches and the unlimited flow of life waiting to come through you all. Bring your heart, your willingness and your faith, and we will bring the heavens through your hands and theirs. Amen...

March 5 – 12

Angels 57 – 64

Sephira 8

HOD ~ Splendor

Overlighting Archangel

RAPHAEL ~ 'Healer-God'
(Governs with MIKHAEL) Healing, wholeness, alchemy/transformation, harmony, awareness.

---

57 NEMAMIAH
58 YEIALEL
59 HARAHEL
60 MITZRAEL
61 UMABEL
62 IAH-HEL
63 ANAUEL
64 MEHIEL

* Note that the Archangel correspondences in Sephirot 6 and 8 have been interchanged throughout the centuries by different Kabbalists and schools of thought. After additional research which shows the ways in which both Archangels are active in both Sephirot, the primary Archangel correspondences presented in the original *Birth Angels* book are reversed here, but each are included as co-governing.

5/17 * 8/1 * 10/14 * 12/25 * **3/5**

57 NEMAMIAH

(neh-MA-mee-YAH)

Discernment (R)

'One who sees through the eyes of the heart'

Archangel ~ RAPHAEL (with MIKHAEL)

Capricorn / Uranus (1/1-5)

I AM THAT WHICH...

helps you to look through the wisdom-eyes of your heart to see that there is more to people, circumstances and events that only love and compassion can see or understand. In bringing your personal discernment to group and mass consciousness, it is helpful to hang back from an instant opinion or reaction to anything that happens. That is because most everyone will likely be instantly reacting – which does not allow a clear vision of the truth-at-hand. That said, reactions are often clues to underlying factors and bigger pictures – so if you are NOT reacting, then you will be able to see beneath the surface the cause and effect of what is truly going on! In a space of non-judging observation your resources of heart-seeing, intuition, empathy and wisdom will be fully available to you. Then, if you are in a position to do so, you will know how to be of help to the group because you will see what their real concerns are – which may be very different from what they say or admit to. And you will understand that everyone needs to get something of what they want in order to be willing to cooperate with the others.

The heart-seeing of discernment is the way of the Divine Feminine in all forms which knows the soul of each and all as her own. She is the seeing of the compassionate Christ-heart and the Quan Yin, the open-petaled purity of the emerging lotus, the welcoming grace of the Shakti mother, the wisdom of Sophia, the

Shekinah of all-embracing love rooted on Earth. When you practice discernment rather than judgment, you amplify the warmth and compassion of the feminine which holds the possibility of all things and beings. When you practice discernment, you are bringing love to thought, wisdom to knowing and compassion for the beingness of life. When you practice discernment, you are the child of wisdom born from the marriage of love and truth, visible and alive, cradled and celebrated from one heart to another, and another.

Therefore my discerning one, draw from my love-light elixir as NEMAMIAH to be love's eyes, love's knowing, love's life and love itself. Lift up your fellow beings with the compassion and understanding that is possible through love's wisdom. Thus may seeming separateness and the lies of fear and doubt be transformed by the love that reveals a more whole and 'truer' truth. So be it. So be it. Amen...

5/18 * 8/2 * 10/15 * 12/26 * **3/6**

58 YEIALEL

(YAY-a-LEL)

Mental Force (R)

'One who lightens the heart to empower mind'

Archangel ~ RAPHAEL (with MIKHAEL)

Capricorn / Saturn (1/6-10)

I AM THAT WHICH...

helps you to have the mental fortitude to implement actions which can bring the purity of a loving truth into beneficial manifestation, and to move forward with difficult endeavors and courses of action that are true and right in the present time for the greater good. When you set about to do good things in your world, you do not necessarily encounter 'greased wheels' and open arms. Sometimes doing good things upsets a lot of 'apple carts' and turns over a lot of tables that have been set with elite place cards for only a few by-invitation-only diners. Therefore you will have to be ready – not for a battle, because battles are distracting – but for unrelenting determination. That means you will need to have a clear and unencumbered heart so as to not take any obstacle personally – whether that obstacle is a person, circumstance, time or a brick wall. And you will need to exercise as much integrity in your means as for your goal. When the naysayers finally realize that you are unstoppable, then your admirers – who may have been watching from the sidelines to see how serious you are – will line up to join you.

If you want to be a good-news creator and conveyor of higher principles in your world, you will have to be strong, joyful and light-footed enough to wade through a lot of sticky attitudes and bad news – because sour grapes and bad news are often more popular! Not because people like negativity or bad news, but because it often makes them feel less bad about their own lives. And we say this with the utmost love and compassion. For if you can keep going, you will inspire not only those in your close circle, but hundreds and possibly even thousands and millions of your brother and sister fellow beings – and crack open a seed of recognition within their hearts that what you are doing is what they want to do and be too, in their own ways.

And so, dear brave-heart, call upon my YEIALEL force within you not to force, but to support your visionary quest and manifest your good works. Bring me your heart when it is disheartened, and I will fill it up with the resiliency of love. Bring me your vulnerability and I will show you your strength. Bring me any fear, doubt or worry – and I will transform them into faith, wisdom and courage. Bring me your dreams and ideals and I will help you turn them into deeds accomplished. Bring me yourself, and I will amplify the Divinity that powers your Divine-Human beingness so that you may know Who you gift and glorify with all you do through the generosity and greatness of your humanity. Amen...

5/19 + 20am * 8/3 * 10/16 * 12/27am * **3/7**

59 HARAHEL

(HA-ra-HEL)

Intellectual Richness (R)

'One who taps feeling and wisdom to enrich mind'

Archangel ~ RAPHAEL (with MIKHAEL)

Capricorn / Jupiter (1/11-15)

I AM THAT WHICH...

helps you to flourish in endeavors which call for higher-mindedness and the ability to draw from diverse thought, wisdom, experiences and peoples in order to expand and heighten creative potential. 'Higher mind' is what your mind can be when it is infused with the greater knowing of heart-wisdom that results from combining knowledge and experience with the creation energy of love. A heart-amplified mind enables you to think beyond the restrictions of time, familiarity and factual observation in order to 'fish for' any potentials that are still making their way from the eternal (where all things already exist) into time. This also enables you to see cause and effect and underlying possibility in people, ideas and situations which do exist in time. Higher mind is a mind at supercharged capacity – like the difference between being mono-visioned and omni-visioned – giving you a 360-degree awareness. With this, you can see how each diverse part contributes to the whole and how the whole can help to bring even more potential within the parts into manifestation.

With this kind of holistic sensibility, you can perceive the impact of actions before they are undertaken and the probabilities among all possibilities. Because higher-mindedness shows you how to juggle and organize many different factors, you will be able to bring together the diversity of people and talent to turn the ideal of cooperation and unity into a working model. This is because higher-mindedness works within the rich and fluid paradigm of inclusivity rather than exclusivity.

Thus, you will especially understand: (1) in order for people to cooperate, everyone needs to be getting something that they need, and there is more than any one way for that to happen without taking it from each other; (2) diversity strengthens, not weakens or dilutes – because each different thing brings something that the others don't have. These two things make for a richer, more multi-faceted whole in which all configurations of beingness, creativity and expression are possible, and the capacities of each within the whole are expanded.

And so dear high, deep and far-thinking one, I give you freely my HARAHEL light that you might bring even greater height, depth and visionary seeing to your ideas and endeavors and be an example for others to do the same. Most people want to reach higher and farther – they just don't know how to, and that's what defeats them before they even start. With our combined light we can show that it's not so much what you already know as what you are willing to learn that ultimately illuminates the 'how.' For when one is willing, the heart's resources come into play, giving access to the eternal – which brings infinite possibility, confidence and enthusiasm. And that's all you need to be off and running! So be it! Amen...

5/20pm + 21 * 8/4 * 10/17 * 12/27pm * **3/8**

60 MITZRAEL

(MITS-ra-EL)

Internal Reparation (R)

'One who repairs what is torn'

Archangel ~ RAPHAEL (with MIKHAEL)

Capricorn / Mars (1/16-20)

I AM THAT WHICH...

helps you to see the ruptures and divisiveness in the world as internal hurts coming to the surface which need healing, and to know how you may do your part to contribute to that healing. Each individual is a generative seed of humanity. What you create in your life creates more or less of the whole. Together, you can add up to a sum greater than your number because of the way energies compound each other. Therefore, in order to repair the collective of humanity, the humans that compose it must be made whole, starting with yourself. That said, it is often hard to see things up close, especially if they are things you don't want to see – so it's easier to focus on what is wrong with the world. So you can start with the world and work your way back to yourself. If you'd like to try that, then we suggest that every time something in the world bothers you, identify what it is and then look to see if there is something similar in your own life. Something you might be thinking, feeling, harboring, exhibiting or suffering in your own actions, circumstances or relatings.

Perhaps the thing that is most 'broken' in your world and which underlies almost all hurt, hate and fear is the inability to embrace diversity. Consider that the fear of differences in others is based on the fear of your own differences and that at any time you might lose your place of belonging. There is even a skewed thought with many that if you ostracize those who are not of your own 'tribe,' your own tribe-identity will be more secure. For diversity to be embraced in your societies, you must appreciate your own differences as part of your unique value to the world – and stop comparing and judging yourself when you don't agree or 'fit in,' or when you don't want to follow the crowd and prefer to 'do it your way.'

You are not here to be the same as any other, but to 'make a difference in the world with your differences.' Thus, focus on the contributions your own and all differences can bring to the whole to make it richer, more interesting and with more opportunity for all – and certainly more peace. You are all brothers and sisters catching the light from different branches on the same tree of life!

I, the MITZRAEL light of the Divine that I Am, tell you that what is 'wrong with the world' or any community, group or organization, is 'wrong' with those who populate it. So if you want to fix your world, fix yourself. And dear one, this is not said in admonishment or judgment, since from our light-perspectives of love and truth, we consider ALL experiences to be catalysts for learning and creating through the 'rub' of contrast that is only possible in duality. For on this Earth, duality is your sandbox, and contrast is how you ultimately make 'sandcastles' or 'sandstorms' of your time and place! It is your choice – though one choice may give you everything you want, and the other only what you need. Either way, there are no losers. Amen...

5/22 * 8/5 * 10/18 * 12/28 * **3/9**

61 UMABEL

(OO-ma-BEL)

Affinity and Friendship (R)

'One who thrums the threads of interconnectedness'

Archangel ~ RAPHAEL (with MIKHAEL)

Aquarius / Sun (1/21-25)

I AM THAT WHICH...

quickens the power of your heart to create common ground between different ideas, peoples, paths and purposes. As we never tire of saying, underneath your beautiful diversities of culture, creed, language, appearance, talents, preferences, work, ways and more, there is a deep sameness of heart. Who among you does not want to love and be loved? Who does not desire to discover and express more of who you truly are? Who doesn't long, even secretly, to offer something meaningful to the world from your own unique talents and interests? Who doesn't wish fulfillment and happiness for your children? It is my honored and sacred task to show you these samenesses of longing and caring which you share, and to help your individual and collective hearts build bridges of friendship that reflect the things which you and all deeply value.

There is great joy in discovering your affinities with others – especially when you or they seem to be very different on the surface. This gives you a sense of belonging that goes beyond your existing circles of familiarity to the realization that you belong in the world, and that the world 'out there' is not a foreign thing to be feared. When a 'stranger' becomes your friend, your brother or sister – even for a moment's meeting – this can transform the way you experience all those who have long been familiar to you and everyone you meet thereafter.

The histories and daily lives of your humanity are full of just such stories. Two 'tech geniuses' on different sides of the world bring their combined expertise to create an innovative product. Two musicians from the east and west make beautiful and unique music together from their combined cultures. Two mothers from different races share the same concern for their sick or hurt children. An elder person and a child comfort each other's vulnerabilities. Two 'enemies' in the heat of war come face to face, and despite their ideological duties let each other pass unharmed. A delay disrupts your schedule, and as you are thwarted from doing or going and forced to be right where you are, you connect with the person next to you who gives you a timely gift of wisdom – even someone who becomes a lifelong friend.

Dear one, thus does my UMABEL light dwell in affinity with and within you, that your earthly affinities may blossom from the understanding that it takes all of your unique hue-manities to detail and 'color in' the ever-expanding bigger picture of life. For it is your sameness of heart that enables you to ***live*** *the bigger picture that you each carry a piece of within your heart and soul. Each time you greet another in friendship, you fill in a little more of the picture within you and on Earth. That is your gift to each other, and all you need is the heart to receive it. So may it be, dear ones, that you may know the joy of universal belonging. Amen...*

5/23 * 8/6 * 10/19 * 12/29 * **3/10**

62 IAH-HEL

(EE-a-HEL)

Desire to Know (R)

'One who calls you to the unknown'

Archangel ~ RAPHAEL (with MIKHAEL)

Aquarius / Venus (1/26-30)

I AM THAT WHICH...

helps to awaken curiosity and interest in other people, ways and ideas that are different from yours and to be open to new encounters and experiences without bias, assumption, suspicion or preconceived opinions. Without fear of the unfamiliar or unknown, you are free to learn about each other's ways of being and living without having your own threatened. In areas where you disagree you can be open to discussion and have the chance to practice humor and patience. When common ground is not immediately apparent, without fear you will seek it. Gone will be the need for others to be the same as you. And in its place will grow a rich diversity of feeling, thought and experience – with new influences and inspirations for creativity and new skies of possibility within yourself and in cooperation and collaboration.

But you should know that for anything you desire or are able to know, there is always more to know. Sometimes you have barely skimmed the surface of knowing when you somehow decide there is nothing more 'there' to know. But know this: unless you are exploring with your heart – as well as your mind – your perception, knowledge and experience will be limited. This is because your heart has greater powers for knowing, seeing and feeling that are beyond time and place, and it sorts information differently. The heart, as repository for and broadcaster of your soul and its truths and purposes, has access to omniscience – an eternal all-knowing which is that of the Divine Itself. And so, with heart-knowing, your thought-perspectives become wider, deeper, higher and farther. You can see what has not been revealed and hear what has not been said. And at the same time, you avoid the pride of knowing and retain the humility and enthusiasm that enables you to know more and more. For as long as your ***desire*** *to know is vibrant, that which can be known will ultimately reveal itself to you.*

The youth among you, unless they have been adulterated by prevailing fears around them, are naturally curious and wanting to know everything – especially what is different from them. And that is what the rest of you love and delight about them. And so let the children be your teachers, to remind you of the great joy you once had for discovery, and to keep the child within you vibrant and contributing to your life. For I tell you as the IAH-HEL light that quickens your appetite for knowing, let not your curiosity about the world wane, no matter your age or circumstance. Keep your inner enthusiasm alive until your very last Earth-breath – and I promise you will take your ability to be amazed with you as you discover with wonder how much more there is still to know! Amen...

5/24 * 8/7 * 10/20 * 12/30 * **3/11**

63 ANAUEL

(a-NA-oo-EL)

Perception of Unity (S)

'One who sees the Oneness within the many'

Archangel ~ RAPHAEL (with MIKHAEL)

Aquarius / Mercury (1/31-2/4)

I AM THAT WHICH...

helps you to see the essential threads of connection and spiritual kinship between yourself and others, and to understand physical separateness as the opportunity for individuation within the greater reality of unity. Unity is without beginning or end and exists as the ever-expanding 'I AM' that is the Divine Author and Totality of life. The context of physical life is a gift that your soul chooses in order to manifest its Divine qualities and purposes in human life and beingness. And courageously, each time you come to Earth, you choose the forgetting of this so that you may experience the challenge of remembering your soul-self in the context of new life situations and variables. What you call 'ego' protects the sovereignty of your human will, and is a co-creative partner with the Divine I AM which your soul comes to Earth to express particular aspects of. However, when you become so preoccupied with your human life that you forget your soul purposes, then your consciousness becomes more identified with your separate human (ego) self than your soul self.

Living with separate-consciousness, as if unity does not exist, does not change the fact that it does – it only deprives you of partaking of the strength, wisdom and power of the greater whole. With separate-consciousness you are confined to the resources of this world and the limits of time. You are 'born alone and die alone,' and it's 'every man for himself' in between. With unity-consciousness, 'no man is an island,' and whatever help or hurt done to one is done to all. You may live as seemingly separate leaves on humanity's family tree of life, each catching the light in your own ways – but it is the tree itself which sustains you. Thus, when you tap the resources of unity, you can draw from the eternal well of omniscience held within your soul and the souls of all others to aid you with matters in time and 'super-charge' your awareness, knowledge and experience.

There is often a push and pull in human thought between the concepts of unity and separation, as if they are mutually exclusive or that separation is an illusion or a 'bad' thing. We would like to shed some light on that. ***The human life of your Divine soul is about the paradox of living in both contexts at once – in which the 'format' of separateness exists within the greater reality, or wholeness, of unity****. You might ask then, what is the purpose of 'separateness if everything is all one anyway?'*

And so we tell you this: so that you may have the gift of time and space 'to do it your way!' Separateness allows a context for the differentiation of Oneness and the cultivation of unique potential through relationship. Just as Oneness is the contextual 'backdrop' for Divine differentiation, so it is also for humanity. Here you each are, as a soul-spark of the Divine Oneness in time, in a unique physical vehicle with the paradoxical Divine-Human purpose to ***indivi****duate particular aspects of what is essentially* ***indivi****sible (the Oneness). Thereby both you and the Divine and all that IS may continually evolve and expand in the fulfillment of your shared Divinely-Human potential.*

And so, while separateness of form is the context of the physical plane – it is not the context of your soul. Thus, your lifelong challenge is to not become so identified with your physical separateness that you forget your soul and the unity which you are essentially part and expressive of. Your bridge to remembering is your heart, which is the broadcaster of your true soul purposes, the place where love and wisdom help you to bring them into being, and the place within where you can see others as your brothers and sisters in unity.

You do not have to always feel unity to be committed to it in awareness and attitude – just as in your partnering and parenting relationships you may not have feelings of love at every moment, even though you are committed to the context of that love. Commitment is key, because while feelings fluctuate, commitment holds a space of constancy in which awareness, feelings and togetherness can be renewed.

My light as ANAUEL is within you to guide you 'back' to the memory of unity which is held within your heart and soul. We know that separateness gives you both pleasure and pain – pleasure in your unlimited opportunities for relationship, creativity and individuation, and pain in the sense of aloneness that comes with the forgetting of your Divine nature and a longing for 'home' and true family. ***Here is the resolution to the paradox: When you learn to embrace both unity and individuation as two sides of the Divine-Human 'coin' that you are, so to speak, you will discover the joy of your differences without feeling separate.***

Remembering the truth of your Divine soul nature and your greater existence in and as part of the All is not permanent, but daily renewable. And this renewal happens whenever you meet another at the heart. Thus may your sense of aloneness be transformed into 'all-oneness' when you see and feel that you are unique sister-brother hues in the great spectrum of 'hue-manity' – making the One knowable, feelable and loveable between, among and as you. Amen...

5/25 * 8/8 * 10/21 * 12/31 * **3/12**

64 MEHIEL

(MAY-hee-EL)

Vivification (Invigorate & Enliven) (G)

'One who brings the elixir of life to the vessel'

Archangel ~ RAPHAEL (with MIKHAEL)

Aquarius / Moon (2/5-9)

I AM THAT WHICH...

helps you to receive and convey to others the enlivening that comes through the universal languages of heart and soul and the vibrancy of inner life making its way to the outer. There is nothing more precious about life than feeling fully alive! Full aliveness allows you to feel and see and know everything in 'high definition.' Every moment becomes a discovery of life and the layers of essence that animate it and you and all. Even in the respite of stillness you can feel the hum of energies revving up for new expressions and essence beginning to fashion itself into new forms. And whether conveyed through art, music, words, innovative ideas or communion with another and the gift of being utterly present in listening and receiving – it is always about bringing the eternal into time, the life-urge into being and doing, and love into creations that live on and on.

There is nothing that gives life more aliveness than love and its powers of boundless expansion and creativity. And there's nothing love loves to expand more than the truth of someone or something – and there's nothing truth loves more than to be expanded! Think about moments in your own life when you realize a truth about yourself or you have a thought, feeling or idea that seems utterly true to you. What happens next? You feel your heart quicken, a sudden excitement, even a catching of your breath, a 'lightbulb moment' in which you may discern patterns and purposes – and then, your creative wheels start turning! That's love in motion, doing its favorite thing, which is to move truth forward into the world. And like a snowball gathering more snow as it rolls down a hill – truth becomes a bigger and bigger truthness because of the love that carries it and all those in its path who come alive in wholeheartedness because of it.

Thus dear alive one, vibrating with infinite potential (whether you always feel it or not), let my MEHIEL light awaken your Divine soul within your humanity and feel and do and be full aliveness. Love, listen and see with heart, and let us be born to the world through you, with you and as you 'on the wings of love.' Let love's aliveness live in your partnerships, friendships, work, projects and collaborations as your energy and enthusiasm are stoked and expanded. Feel the 'bigger-than-life' forces of fruitful togetherness that magnify and extend each person's best qualities, talents and abilities! Let our two worlds be commingled and our co-creations be evidence of the Heavens on Earth and in your collective hearts, where love comes to put down roots and blossom into all you can be individually and together. So be it with you and us and all. Amen...

March 13 –20

Angels 65 – 72

Sephira 9

YESOD ~ Foundation

Overlighting Archangel

GABRIEL ~ 'God is my Strength'
Guidance, vision, inspiration for faith
and connection to the Divine; vessel for
giving and receiving, creative fertility,
and the ebb and flow of life's seasons

---

65 DAMABIAH
66 MANAKEL
67 EYAEL
68 HABUHIAH
69 ROCHEL
70 JABAMIAH
71 HAIYAEL
72 MUMIAH

5/26 * 8/9 * 10/22 * 1/1 * **3/13**

65 DAMABIAH

(da-MA-bee-YAH)

Fountain of Wisdom (R)

'One who brings the ocean to the river'

Archangel ~ GABRIEL

Aquarius / Uranus (2/10-14)

I AM THAT WHICH...

helps you to contribute your wisdom to the world in a way that is inclusive, transformative and ennobling of individuals while encouraging heartful awareness and a sense of unity and cooperation. Wisdom is intrinsically holistic – it has a 'bigger-picture' perspective that includes not only the values held by one's own self, but a sense of the self as part of the greater whole which encompasses the interests and well-being of others. The person who is guided by wisdom in any endeavor, field or industry knows that to work in a way which depletes any person or group will ultimately undermine all. Thus, wisdom undertakes projects and endeavors with motives and methods that display integrity and commitment to higher principles and the impact upon all. While wisdom in practice is heartful and inclusive, it is also mindful and discerning about long-term goals and mutual sustainability. Wisdom considers all factors for a best outcome that brings thriving to individuals and also to the whole in a way that provides an ongoing context for continued mutual support.

Wisdom is a powerful ally in your world. Wisdom is fluid and infinitely creative, so when it 'hits a wall' it finds another way – through the cracks, around it, or dissolving it with diplomacy, respect, kindness and affirmative strategies. Wisdom understands seasons, cycles and underlying aspects, and is willing to lose sometimes so that other things can be won. Wisdom knows that there is more to time than the ticking, spending or passing of it, and that every thing and being comes to fruition in its own due course – which is not clock-time but eternal time – not a duration, but a quality of being. Wisdom accepts what-is while still striving toward what can be, because wisdom knows that nothing is impossible unless you believe it to be.

My wisdom-light as DAMABIAH tells you these things: there is a sacred purpose for every being, for each expresses an aspect of the Divine on Earth. To war over your differences is to war with yourselves and the Divine within and among you, even as your 'auto-immune' diseases war against your own body and being. The ills in your world will not be healed by violence, because acts and energies of destruction only beget more of the same. The tides of hurt and hate, greed, encroachment and ideological extremism can only be stemmed by the powers of love and the recognition that truth dwells within and is inclusive to all beings, in different ways.

Thus, dear wisdom-making one, if your world would be wise, then you and each must bring your personal wisdom to it. Just as wisdom is cultivated within by bringing knowledge and experience into your heart – where they are transformed into a greater knowing by love – so must you bring the events of your world into your collective hearts so that you will know how to heal them. So be it. Amen...

5/27 * 8/10 * 10/23 * 1/2 * **3/14**

66 MANAKEL

(MA-na -KEL)

Knowledge of Good and Evil (R)

'One who lights a candle to cure the darkness'

Archangel ~ GABRIEL

Aquarius / Saturn (2/15-19)

I AM THAT WHICH...

helps you to come together in cooperation to realize that all play a part in the hurt or healing of your world, and that in order to rehabilitate what is destructive, all must rise beyond blame to contribute to healing. Often after negative events in your world there is much time spent on trying to determine who's to blame rather than who will step up to help course-correct – as if being part of the solution will somehow admit to responsibility for the problem. We tell you this – there is never one cause of any 'bad act.' The need to narrow the field of blame and hold someone accountable is often driven by the need to 'put an end to the matter' and restore some sense of absolution and safety to everyone else.

Understand this, with love and compassion, as we do: most acts of 'evil' are focused eruptions from an imbalance or distortion within the whole which has manifested in an aberration of a part. For example, a society which chronically ignores or causes hurt or disenfranchisement to particular peoples will ultimately yield individuals who will prey on that society. Tyrannical groups or governments bring about civil wars and genocide. Those who are rejected or feel an unbelonging in their social or religious groups may use distorted ideologies to spawn 'acts of terror' across the world that are funded, fueled and armed by those seeking recognition, power, money and control. Despite the tendency to isolate 'acts of evil' as the doings of deranged or immoral others, there is always something in the whole of a society – sometimes initiated generations earlier – which contributes to the bad acts of individuals or self-interested groups. And it is not because of some notion of 'original sin' – but because in the duality of life, you have the free will to go toward creation **or** *destruction in your quest to experience and learn from all the shades of life as you explore your soul purposes.*

We do not say these things to admonish or instill shame – but to illuminate that in the paradigm of Oneness all play a part in everything that was, is and will be – and it is your choice as to which part you will play. Know this from my light-knowledge as MANAKEL: each time a 'darkness' is expressed in your world, it does so because of its innate longing to be included in the light; thus, to heal darkness, do not fight it – but rather, BE LIGHT. Thereby you will join the Angelic forces of light within and among you to use the eruptions of 'evil' as a signal to marshal the great powers of Love and Truth to show where healing is needed. Be comforted to know that acts of evil have an inherent finiteness, but the compassion and forgiveness you can meet them with ripple out forever as waves of awakened love throughout humanity and the cosmos. Thus, be Love, and the light will expand into the dark until the dark itself is light. Amen...

5/28 * 8/11 * 10/24 * 1/3 * **3/15**

67 EYAEL

(AY-ya -EL)

Transformation to the Sublime (R)

'One who illumines the inner star'

Archangel ~ GABRIEL

Pisces / Jupiter (2/20-24)

I AM THAT WHICH...

helps you to contribute your personal soul-awareness and higher consciousness into group and community in order to uplift and preserve 'the soul of the world.' The physical world of matter and manifestation is continually animated and supported by the essential energies of the spiritual world – just as your human vehicle is supported by the Divine Essence carried in your soul, along with your breath and heartbeat which support your body waking or sleeping. This is the inner supporting the outer, which is naturally in play from the minutest to the grandest creations.

Your personal inner is automatically 'bundled' with your 'birth package' – involuntary to your human aspects, but voluntary to your soul, since it is your soul that volunteered itself to come to Earth. By virtue of the soul within your humanity, you have both conscious and unconscious access to the eternal realms of Divine Essence and cosmic consciousness. What this provides for your human experience is a way to enliven, enhance and even surpass, the physical and mental capacities – and limitations – of form, fact, time, place, the five senses, and so on. It is only when these finite aspects of your humanity are imbued with the meaning, purpose and omniscient energies carried by your soul – that your heart, mind and body can fulfill their higher potentials to 'super-charge' your life.

Just as you have the power to hold your breath or to breathe less or more, deeper or shallower – it is your choice of how much you are willing to co-create with your own soul energies and resources. Sure, you can put up barriers of thought and attitude that keep you from partaking, and living, fully. But you literally have the Divine 'on tap' in the well of your own soul – and it's always an 'open bar!'

My EYAEL light within you is given so that you may fill any thought, feeling, thing or happening in your life with the 'sublime' resources of your soul and its spiritual lifeline to the eternal and infinite Divine. You are a light-wand in a world that needs every spiritual 'abracadabra' you can wield! Imagine what may be conjured when your light-powers are multiplied by the many! Imagine 'mass consciousness' that is truly conscious rather than unconscious. Imagine 'crowd mentality' that becomes 'crowd spirituality,' generated from within and among each and all for the greater and highest good of everyone's inner and outer, no exclusions.

What sublime thing would you like to join me in bringing to the world today that might inspire even one other person to a higher and more joyful experience of living? A smile perhaps? A listening ear, a comforting shoulder, a next-step-up for their dream? A plan for eradicating world hunger or to ensure that every child has the chance for an education, starting with your neighbor? It is entirely your choice – the choice of your ego-self and your soul-self, working and creating in collaboration. So may it be, so may you co-create and uplift the world with the sublime that is always within you. Amen...

5/29 * 8/12 * 10/25 * 1/4 * **3/16**

68 HABUHIAH

(ha-BU-hee-YAH)

Healing (R)

'One who loves hurt into healing'

Archangel ~ GABRIEL

Pisces / Mars (2/25-29)

I AM THAT WHICH...

helps you to heal your world by understanding the hurts that continue to persist as guides to where healing is needed, and by learning from the Earth how to lean into what is light-and-life-affirming and tap your inner resiliencies to be reborn again and again. Do you want to be part of the healing of your world? It is natural to want to turn away from the hurting of the masses to find some personal joy in your own life (which has hurts enough). Yet, as we have said in so many ways throughout our communications, when you heal yourself you contribute to the healing of the world.

Your local and global news is often just "bad news on top of bad.' Wisdom will tell you that there are many causal threads that have contributed to all the hurts that persist within you and all of humankind. In the cumulative effect of doing unto others, including the Earth itself and what has been done to you (rather than 'as you would have them do unto you') – you are all part of the cause, and thus, part of the cure.

Sometimes you don't want to know because knowledge can cause you to despair or feel shame that you are not doing enough. But if you see the bad news as revelations of what and where the hurt is, you can participate in the healing that is needed – and perhaps without even leaving your couch! By recognizing your own hurt in the hurt of the world, you can bring your heart-

consciousness with compassion and healing intent toward yourself and all by feeling the 'we' that you are part of – and realizing that there is no 'them' that you are not part and expressive of.

Nature is self-healing in many ways, which means that it intrinsically knows what it needs, and all its parts make adjustments as the strong strengthen the weak in order to restore health and wholeness. Humans have the same natural intelligence, but what you have that nature doesn't is reason – and unreason! While your mind is a highly-developed organizer, it can also run interference in ways that do not contribute to healing. You must return to your own soul nature, which is akin to the nature of the natural world – and you will remember how to heal.

Thus, come with me and my healing HABUHIAH light to walk among nature's trees, which symbolize the cosmic Tree of Life and its mysteries of creation and wholeness. However bare-boned trees may seem in their winter season, they are silently and deeply re-gathering energies to bring forth the new totality of themselves in the Spring. They naturally know how to rebirth their form from their essence again and again. So come and tell them where the hurt is in you and your world. Start the conversation from your heart, for they understand feeling. Listen to the wisdoms they are waiting to share with you, and let go of the hurts they are willing to absorb so that you might walk lighter – and thereby make your world lighter. Let the trees and all of nature's growing things show you how to take in more and more light by drawing it from your innermost resources of heart, soul and Divine-rootedness. And finally, draw in the breath of the Earth itself, breathing for you and with you, for you and with you, always. Amen...

5/30 * 8/13 * 10/26 * 1/5 * **3/17**

69 ROCHEL

(ro-SHEL)

Restitution (R)

'One who brings back your lost parts'

Archangel ~ GABRIEL

Pisces / Sun (3/1-5)

I AM THAT WHICH...

helps to restore what has been lost or stolen by the marginalization of personal values and any infringement against your or others' rights to pursue a life of meaning, purpose and fulfillment. One of the vital things that often 'slips between the cracks' in organizations, corporations and governments is personal values and ideals. When the standards of integrity and well-being you would want for yourself and your loved ones are missing from the bottom lines of what you create in the world, then you are stealing something from yourself, your loved ones – and all.

Restitution is not about revenge or punishment. It is about restoring what was taken, not allowed or not rightly given. You are born with the Divine birthright to make of your life what you will and to be free to pursue your soul purposes and heart's desires. If you find yourself on this Earth in a situation that prohibits, or at the very least does not support, those rights, then you have two choices – continue to live with those constraints and work with the lessons and gifts within them – or use your creativity, integrity and resolve to restore the life-affirming opportunities that have been denied to you and others.

Sometimes you may think your work or life condition is just 'the way it is' – especially if your family, community or country are living in limiting circumstances. But the truer, more loving and bigger picture view is: 'this is showing where healing and change are needed.'

Dear one, if you are living in an environment that is not equitable and supportive of your values and your blossoming as a Divine-Human being, you have the Divine light you need inside to rehabilitate your environment or plant yourself and your seeds of hopes and dreams in different soil – starting with the cultivation of your own inner 'humus' with seeds of higher consciousness. If you are in a situation from which you cannot extricate yourself quite yet, you can begin to change your conditions by changing how you relate to them and how you let them affect you, or not. Tremendous dignity is born of this because you come to realize that you have so much more power within you than your circumstances have allowed you to feel. For just from changing your thought, your awareness and your willingness, shift will begin to happen.

Therefor is my light as ROCHEL given unto you, to help you focus not on what seems impossible, but what is possible right where you are, right now. There is always a next step waiting to be taken, and always someone or something in both the physical and eternal realms that will meet you there. The same thing goes for encouraging and helping others who are in limiting circumstances. You may not be able to change their 'locale,' but you can certainly help and inspire them to change the way they experience it. By helping to illuminate and awaken their inner resources of intuition, creativity and personal truth, they will have access to every next step needed to change their lives. We say to you and all – ***believe in your heart's desires, not your life's circumstances****. For the truth is that life on Earth is a limiting circumstance! But you can reclaim unlimitedness at any time from within you! Amen...*

5/31 * 8/14 * 10/27 * 1/6 * **3/18**

70 JABAMIAH

(ya-BA-mee-YAH)

Alchemy (Transformation) (R)

'One who turns base mettle into gold'

Archangel ~ GABRIEL

Pisces / Venus (3/6-10)

I AM THAT WHICH...

helps you to bring forth new growth and possibility by harnessing the hidden energies of transformation in the changing of the seasons and cycles of the natural world, as well as in your own being and in the world around you. The processes of change are always cycling from beginning to end and another new beginning, which is how life expands and moves forward. Big and loud change is exciting – but it is the transitional times when not much seems to be happening that the most formative and even spectacular things are occurring below the surface. These are the times of alchemical change – when essence becomes form and form begins to differentiate and expand. This is when the first submerged tendril of new growth is pushing its way up through dark soil to the warming surface, while its roots are burrowing toward moisture and nutrients in the depths. And it is when a 'seedling' in the womb progresses from a dot to a wonder of differentiated details of tissue and bone. This energy of potential new aliveness is always in the within of everything, including yourself, waiting for its due time to burst forth. You must also realize that your times of transformation can be your most fragile. Thus to prepare for any birthing, you must allow sufficient gestation time in order to gather strength of purpose from within – and be mindful to pick your time and place of emergence in a "friendly" atmosphere, if possible.

To bring about profound change in the fruits you reap in your life, you must plant different seeds. Thoughts and feelings are the seeds of all relatings, conditions and circumstances. But these are sometimes undermined or overruled by fixed ideas that have become beliefs. Thus if you want to change your life, you must allow your thoughts and feelings an uncluttered space to flow and process beyond the boundaries of belief. Beliefs organize your thoughts and feelings into what is familiar, 'acceptable' or relatable, whereas thoughts and feelings can lead you into the umknown and potentially a pure and direct line to your inner Divine and greater knowing.

Much of the divisiveness in your world revolves around disagreements about beliefs and belief systems. And all too often, it is adherence to a belief system which has kept you separate and disempowered from relationship with your inner Divine. The functions of organizational belief systems have supposedly been to deter chaos and to protect against potentially distorted or rampant thoughts or passions, as well as the uncertainties of life. However, this ultimately shows a mistrust of your birthright and ability to co-create your life with the Divine that dwells within you.

You are always secretly or overtly changing. It is the seeming involuntary changes that often bring about the greatest transformation – because these are choices for change which you make at the soul level – even though your human personality might be resisting! Thus may you draw from my JABAMIAH elixir of alchemical light to increase the flow of your Divine soul-light into the love-and-wisdom-cup of your heart, and from that innermost altar into your mind and body. Remember that you are a seed of humanity, and your own transformation will help to transform humanity itself. Be saturated with your own light, and keep company with the light of others so that together the whole world may be lit from the withins of all. And in your greater commingled light, world change will come of its own volition – because one day all things and beings, without exception, will want to be that light. Amen...

6/1 * 8/15 * 10/28 * 1/7 * **3/19**

71 HAIYAEL

(HA-ee-ya-EL)

Divine Warrior & Weaponry (R)

'One who wins the battle that cannot be fought'

Archangel ~ GABRIEL

Pisces / Mercury (3/11-15)

I AM THAT WHICH...

helps to invigorate just causes without a hidden agenda, and to show that true victory comes not with fighting the negative, but supporting and expanding the positive. In the duality of life, people take on positive or negative 'causes' for different positive or negative reasons. With positive causes, some are called from a sense of community and desire to contribute, some to heal a personal tragedy by helping others, and some to fill an emptiness inside them or to muffle feelings of unworthiness by having something external to fight. You can usually tell the difference between these because the first and second are supporting something and will display enthusiasm, a sense of joy and even heightened abilities. The latter is fighting against something and likely walks under a cloud of irritation or despair, often causing disruption of ideas and plans of action. A group is only as strong as its healthiest member. The solution, however, is not to shun the weaker members, but to illuminate the greater light inside them so that they might see the potential of their unique contributions – and then – invite them to shine.

Those who take on negative, as in life-negating, causes – do so for a variety of reasons as well. For some it's about greed and power, while others are driven by a deep sense of deprivation and a desire to quash the forces which they feel exploited by – and still others have embraced beliefs so distorted that the negation of life is seen as a positive, even holy, act. However, we wish you to see that as different and distorted as the values of those who take the life of others may seem from your own values, these are the hurting and hating people in your world who show you where healing is needed within all of you.

I tell you as HAIYAEL that just as those who visit your upper atmospheres can see the blanket of Earth-dweller lights twinkling through the dark, we of the cosmic realms see the inner soul-lights of all humanity radiating from time into eternity. And we tell you that however much darkness may seem to be rampant upon the Earth, it is nothing compared to your combined light. Although it may appear that there are more and more beings in your world warring against each other, there are also more than ever before 'leaning into' the light of love, compassion, peace and harmony.

'Fighting the good fight' should not be a fight at all, but the building of a 'critical mass' of support for the new thing you want to create. All your power lies in expanding the light (what you want) rather than fighting the dark (what you don't want), because the energies of creation are drawn to what you give your attention and focus to. Thus, it is far better to educate each other about your ways than to shoot each other! Far better to bring your neighbors into the light of belonging than to have them prey upon those who exclude them. Better to plant more love than fight with the weeds.

I tell you this as the HAIYAEL Divine Light-warrior that I am: every atrocity is the dark fighting a dying battle as it comes to the surface for its 'last hurrah' of illusion that it is not light – and its secret desire to be so. One day ***every thing and being which has forgotten its own light will be drawn out of the dark to be returned into light consciousness as it cannot help but remember its true nature as love.***

And so, we say to you – do not lose heart with your world – because your Earth, and your heart, are where love has come to put down roots, and the truth is that in the end, as in the beginning, 'love is all there is.' Amen...

6/2 * 8/16 * 10/29 * 1/8 * **3/20**

72 MUMIAH

(MOO-mee-YAH)

Endings and Rebirth (R)

'One who uses endings to begin again'

Archangel ~ GABRIEL

Pisces / Moon (3/16-20)

I AM THAT WHICH...

helps to bring comfort and nurturing while expediting endings and the last letting go in order for you to be unencumbered for a new period of creation, fertility and opportunity. Just as the seed in due time must let go of its shell and the dark earth that has been its womb, at each season's end you too must let go of what was in order to be ready for what will be. The passage between yesterday and a new today is often a dark one, and the fear of that can make some hang back from change. But imagine if there was no dark for the dawn to emerge from? Imagine if a new seedling was afraid to travel through the dark soil to reach the surface? Imagine if a child in the womb did not have the life-urge to travel through the dark birth canal, despite the discomfort, in order to emerge into its new life in the world? Imagine if your own thoughts and feelings did not have their inner gestation time so that new ideas and creations could begin to coalesce and take form from within you?

Transitions are not just something to get through, however uncomfortable, dark and without navigation they seem to be at times. They are a vital part of transformation during which all the last little bits are made ready, both inside you and in the world, for new life to emerge.

How this plays out in your societies is often a reluctance for change, because in order to change a previous way, doctrine, protocol, order, and so on, there is usually a period of chaos so that the old order, or certain parts of it, can be dismantled to make a space for the new. Just as in your personal life, fear arises around losing the familiar and having to learn to reorganize life around something new. This fear is compelling and can psychologically defeat initiative and innovation. But inherent in life itself and every life form, including you, is a built-in instinct to move forward and create anew. Thus, where change is needed, there is always an underlying energetic momentum which has been building – and if there is resistance to that change, it will manifest, if necessary, through other events to force the change. For example, when a natural cataclysm brings a community together which has been divisive or dissociated from the needs and conditions of its citizens. Or when you lose a job you have been afraid to leave, having stayed too long to the detriment of your health and well-being. Or when an impending death in the family brings members together who haven't spoken in years. In each case, an ending has provided a path for a new beginning.

And so, let my light as MUMIAH be your shepherd across the dark bridge from yesterday to a new day. We are with you in every ending, transition and new beginning – for we love to attend you in these creative times! Look at your life in our light, and you will see that as you move forward, though the way be still unclear, you are expanding yourself, the world and all that is Divine. And we promise this – you and your world will move inner and outer mountains if you move with heart. For it is great feeling that can turn each step into a quantum leap, each leap into a new horizon, each horizon into a brand new world. Follow your individual and collective hearts, and 'your feet will always find a road' through what seems to be the most impassable and impenetrable attitudes and conditions. And remember always, you do not have to fight the dark to move forward. You only have to bring the commingled light of love and truth, for together these are the dark's great dissolver. And we shall meet your willingness to be fully alive with our collective Angelic light joined with yours. Amen...

Sephira 10

MALKUTH (SHEKINAH)

Relates to the Kingdom of Creation

and the Realm of Saints and Ascended Souls

Overlighting Archangels

SANDALPHON and METATRON

These two Archangels, sometimes referred to as "spiritual brothers," are arguably said to be the only two Archangels who were once human and taken up to the heavens without having experienced human death: METATRON was Enoch, and SANDALPHON was Elijah. Metatron's unmanifested creation energies in KETHER are finally manifest in MALKUTH and the SHEKINAH (feminine aspect of the Divine) which gives birth to Earth. Thus here METATRON is the link between the Divine and all of humanity, while SANDALPHON is the overlighting Archangel of the Earth and planetary "caretaker" who grounds Divine Love within humanity and the natural world in order to cultivate higher consciousness on Earth.

In the Tree of Life symbology, Sephira 10 is a "bridge" realm leading from the Angelic Heavens to the realm of saints and ascended souls, and ultimately to Earth. Therefore, there are no Angels (except Archangels) correspondent to this last Sephira of the Tree. However, it is included here in order to complete the spiritual descent of the Heavenly Tree of Life unto Earth as it takes root and branches out into, within and among the hearts of all humanity.

Amen...Amen...Amen

Appendix I

Your Personal Birth Angels

The ancient wisdoms reveal that our souls come to Earth for many lifetimes in order to heal the unhealed hurts and issues that occur in human life, which we call our "karma" – thus may we advance the "dharma" of our soul purposes in service to the expansion of the Divine on Earth within ourselves and others. We are made "in the image and likeness" of the Divine because our soul, as a spark of the Divine, is made of Divine "Light-stuff," which imprints the qualities and nature of the Divine within us. The 72 Angels are said to be the "angles" of that Light-stuff which help the Divine to come alive and be activated within us. Thus, it is said that there is a kind of hologram of all 72 Angels that overlights each of us.

In addition, because of the density and forgetfulness of Earth-life, it is said that in our soul-choice of circumstances for each lifetime we also choose certain influences, guides and cosmic aspects around our time of birth that will act as symbols, or "signatures," to remind and support us with what we came here to do. Thus, we are especially attended by the three Angels who were "governing" at the moment we were born, who throughout our lives help to quicken and amplify the spark of Divinity that is our soul and its expression in time, meaning and matter. Our Birth Angels take on these roles as they work with the physical, emotional and mental aspects of our being:

Your **Incarnation Angel** ~ Expresses qualities of the Divine Being and Will through human physical existence, will and life purpose. Corresponds to your five-day period of birth and supports the qualities, challenges and expressions of your physical being and the will to carry out your soul purposes in your human lifetime.

Your **Heart Angel** ~ Expresses qualities of Divine Love through the feelings and wisdoms of the human heart. Corresponds to your actual day of birth, your emotional qualities, challenges and potentials, and supports the cultivation of personal truth and wisdom, as well as love, compassion, forgiveness and understanding for self and others.

Your **Intellect Angel** ~ Expresses qualities of Divine Mind through the constructs and creations of human intelligence. Corresponds to your time of birth (within 20 minutes), your mental qualities, challenges and potentials and the cultivation of greater awareness and higher-mind. Those born at a cusp time (on the hour or 20 minutes before or after) have two Intellect Angels (for a total of four Birth Angels).

Your Birth Angels are those which correspond your day and time of birth to the Angels' days and times of support. However, if your birthdate or time are close to the governing days or times of the Angels just before or after your Birth Angels, then you might want to be guided to those which have the stronger resonance for you.

I would like to clarify the use of the term "govern." The Angels are spoken of as governing certain days and times, as well as the different planes of human beingness (physical, emotional and mental). What is meant by governing is *influence*, *correspondence* and *support*. Ideally, because of our Divinely-endowed birthright of free will, we humans govern ourselves and support each other. The Angels, thus, do not govern us, but bring a positive influence of Divine energies and support for our highest good – which is to amplify the truth of who we each uniquely are and support the fruition of our soul purposes and potentials in both time and eternity.

Degrees/days. Ancient Kabbalists working with the 72 Angels corresponded their hierarchies of governing to 360 degrees of the Zodiac, with each degree ideally correspondent to one day. However, we live in a 365-day solar year. From my research of ancient calendars, it seems that many early civilizations adhered to a lunar calendar of approximately 30 days per month x 12 months = 360 days (the Mayans, for example, which accounts for the discrepancies of dates between then and now). However, Earth's orbit around the sun is elliptical – not a perfect circle – and thus every few years certain civilizations would tack on an extra month to make up the difference between lunar and solar cycles. In 45 B.C., the Julian solar calendar was established, which took us to a 365.25-day year, with a "leap" year every four years. This was reformed by the slightly more accurate Gregorian calendar in 1582. Isaac Newton surmised in 1728 that the original 360-degree Zodiac was attributed to the early widespread use of a 360-day calendar. (www.360dayyear.com and www.en.wikipedia.org/wiki/Julian_calendar). In order to reconcile degrees with days in working with the 72 Angels, some overlapping of dates had to occur to cover all 365/366 days. (I too work with days rather than degrees because they are more universally relatable.)

The 72 Angels' Days of Incarnation Support

Your Incarnation Angel expresses the Divine Being and Will in human physical existence, will and life purpose. Their dates of governing correspond to the five-day period around your birth and the qualities, challenges and expressions of your physical being and purpose:

3/21 - 25 | 1 VEHUIAH – Will & New Beginnings
3/26 - 30 | 2 JELIEL – Love & Wisdom
3/31 – 4/4 | 3 SITAEL – Construction of Worlds
4/5 – 9 | 4 ELEMIAH – Divine Power
4/10 – 14 | 5 MAHASIAH – Rectification
4/15 – 20 | 6 LELAHEL – Light of Understanding
4/21 – 25 | 7 ACHAIAH – Patience
4/26 – 30 | 8 CAHETEL – Divine Blessings
5/1 – 5 | 9 HAZIEL – Divine Mercy & Forgiveness
5/6 – 10 | 10 ALADIAH – Divine Grace
5/11 – 15 | 11 LAUVIAH – Victory
5/16 – 20 | 12 HAHAIAH – Refuge/Shelter
5/21 – 25 | 13 YEZALEL – Fidelity, Loyalty, Allegiance
5/26 – 31 | 14 MEBAHEL – Truth, Liberty, Justice
6/1 – 5 | 15 HARIEL – Purification
6/6 – 10 | 16 HAKAMIAH – Loyalty
6/11 – 15 | 17 LAVIAH – Revelation
6/16 – 21 | 18 CALIEL – Justice
6/22 – 26 | 19 LEUVIAH – Expansive Intelligence, Fruition
6/27 – 7/1 | 20 PAHALIAH – Redemption
7/2 – 6 | 21 NELCHAEL – Ardent Desire to Learn
7/7 – 11 | 22 YEIAYEL – Fame/Renown
7/12 – 16 | 23 MELAHEL – Healing Capacity
7/17 – 22 | 24 HAHEUIAH – Protection
7/23 – 27 | 25 NITH-HAIAH – Spiritual Wisdom & Magic
7/28 – 8/1 | 26 HAAIAH – Political Science & Ambition

8/2 – 6	27 YERATEL – Propagation of the Light
8/7 – 12	28 SEHEIAH – Longevity
8/13 – 17	29 REIYEL – Liberation
8/18 – 22	30 OMAEL – Fertility, Multiplicity
8/23 – 28	31 LECABEL – Intellectual Talent
8/29 – 9/2	32 VASARIAH – Clemency & Equilibrium
9/3 – 7	33 YEHUIAH – Subordination to Higher Order
9/8 – 12	34 LEHAHIAH – Obedience
9/13 – 17	35 CHAVAKIAH – Reconciliation
9/18 – 23	36 MENADEL – Inner/Outer Work
9/24 – 28	37 ANIEL – Breaking the Circle
9/29 – 10/3	38 HAAMIAH – Ritual & Ceremony
10/4 – 8	39 REHAEL – Filial Submission
10/9 – 13	40 YEIAZEL – Divine Consolation & Comfort
10/14 – 18	41 HAHAHEL – Mission
10/19 – 23	42 MIKAEL – Political Authority & Order
10/24 – 28	43 VEULIAH – Prosperity
10/29 – 11/2	44 YELAHIAH – Karmic Warrior
11/3 – 7	45 SEALIAH – Motivation & Willfulness
11/8 – 12	46 ARIEL – Perceiver & Revealer
11/13 – 17	47 ASALIAH – Contemplation
11/18 – 22	48 MIHAEL – Fertility & Fruitfulness
11/23 – 27	49 VEHUEL – Elevation & Grandeur
11/28 – 12/2	50 DANIEL – Eloquence
12/3 – 7	51 HAHASIAH – Universal Medicine
12/8 – 12	52 IMAMIAH – Expiation of Errors
12/13 – 16	53 NANAEL – Spiritual Communication
12/17 – 21	54 NITHAEL – Rejuvenation & Eternal Youth
12/22 – 26	55 MEBAHIAH – Intellectual Lucidity
12/27 – 1/31	56 POYEL – Fortune & Support
1/1 – 5	57 NEMAMIAH – Discernment
1/6 – 10	58 YEIALEL – Mental Force
1/11 – 15	59 HARAHEL – Intellectual Richness
1/16 – 20	60 MITZRAEL – Internal Reparation
1/21 – 25	61 UMABEL – Affinity & Friendship
1/26 – 30	62 IAH-HEL – Desire to Know
1/31 – 2/4	63 ANAUEL – Perception of Unity
2/5 – 9	64 MEHIEL – Vivification (Invigorate/Enliven)

2/10 – 14	65 DAMABIAH – Fountain of Wisdom
2/15 – 19	66 MANAKEL – Knowledge of Good & Evil
2/20 – 24	67 EYAEL – Transformation to Sublime
2/25 – 29	68 HABUHIAH – Healing
3/1 – 5	69 ROCHEL – Restitution
3/6 – 10	70 JABAMIAH – Alchemy (Transformation)
3/11 – 15	71 HAIYAEL – Divine Warrior & Weaponry
3/16 – 20	72 MUMIAH – Endings & Rebirth

The 72 Angels' Times of Intellect Support

The following shows all 72 Angels in their one 20-minute period in the 24-hour day when they are governing the intellect plane, and thus expressing particular qualities of Divine Mind in your human intellect to help you cultivate awareness and higher-mind. Your Intellect Angel is the one that was governing 20 minutes within your time of birth at your place of birth. Thus, if you were born at 12:10 a.m., your Intellect Angel would be 1 VEHUIAH. Those born at a cusp time – on the hour or 20 minutes before or after – have two Intellect Angels; so if you were born at 12:20, your two Intellect Angels would be 1 VEHUIAH and 2 JELIEL – or you may want to work with the one with which you feel the most resonance. Likewise if your time of birth is very close to a cusp time.

Note that there is another system of determining your Intellect Angel that was developed by 20th century Kabbalist, Kabaleb (see Appendix II), from his orientation as an esoteric astrologer in corresponding the 72 Angels to 360 degrees of the Zodiac. With his system you must find out when the sun rose at the exact day, year and place you were born, correspond that to the exact degree of the Zodiac on that date, and then do a complex counting computation, which admittedly, I do not fully understand nor have the resources for. However, I invite you to pursue this if you desire by contacting Kabaleb's son, Tristan Llop (nuevavibracion.com).

Also note that for those who use a 24-hour clock, 12:00 a.m. midnight to 12:00 p.m. noon would be 00:00-12:00, and 12:00 p.m. noon to 12 midnight is 12:00-24:00.

12 Midnight (a.m.) to 12 Noon (p.m.)

(00:00 – 12:00)

Time	Angel
12:00 – 12:20	1 VEHUIAH – Will & New Beginnings
12:20 – 12:40	2 JELIEL – Love & Wisdom
12:40 – 1:00	3 SITAEL – Construction of Worlds
1:00 – 1:20	4 ELEMIAH – Divine Power
1:20 – 1:40	5 MAHASIAH – Rectification
1:40 – 2:00	6 LELAHEL – Light of Understanding
2:00 – 2:20	7 ACHAIAH – Patience
2:20 – 2:40	8 CAHETEL – Divine Blessings
2:40 – 3:00	9 HAZIEL – Divine Mercy & Forgiveness
3:00 – 3:20	10 ALADIAH – Divine Grace
3:20 – 3:40	11 LAUVIAH – Victory
3:40 – 4:00	12 HAHAIAH – Refuge/Shelter
4:00 – 4:20	13 YEZALEL – Fidelity, Loyalty, Allegiance
4:20 – 4:40	14 MEBAHEL – Truth, Liberty, Justice
4:40 – 5:00	15 HARIEL – Purification
5:00 – 5:20	16 HAKAMIAH – Loyalty
5:20 – 5:40	17 LAVIAH – Revelation
5:40 – 6:00	18 CALIEL – Justice
6:00 – 6:20	19 LEUVIAH – Expansive Intelligence, Fruition
6:20 – 6:40	20 PAHALIAH – Redemption
6:40 – 7:00	21 NELCHAEL – Ardent Desire to Learn
7:00 – 7:20	22 YEIAYEL – Fame/Renown
7:20 – 7:40	23 MELAHEL – Healing Capacity
7:40 – 8:00	24 HAHEUIAH – Protection
8:00 – 8:20	25 NITH-HAIAH – Spiritual Wisdom & Magic
8:20 – 8:40	26 HAAIAH – Political Science & Ambition
8:40 – 9:00	27 YERATEL – Propagation of the Light
9:00 – 9:20	28 SEHEIAH – Longevity
9:20 – 9:40	29 REIYEL – Liberation
9:40 – 10:00	30 OMAEL – Fertility, Multiplicity
10:00 – 10:20	31 LECABEL – Intellectual Talent
10:20 – 10:40	32 VASARIAH – Clemency & Equilibrium
10:40 – 11:00	33 YEHUIAH – Subordination to Higher Order
11:00 – 11:20	34 LEHAHIAH – Obedience
11:20 – 11:40	35 CHAVAKIAH – Reconciliation
11:40 – 12:00	36 MENADEL – Inner/Outer Work

12:00 Noon (p.m.) to 12 Midnight (a.m.)

(12:00 – 24:00)

12:00 – 12:20 | 37 ANIEL – Breaking the Circle
12:20 – 12:40 | 38 HAAMIAH – Ritual & Ceremony
12:40 – 1:00 | 39 REHAEL – Filial Submission
1:00 – 1:20 | 40 YEIAZEL – Divine Consolation & Comfort
1:20 – 1:40 | 41 HAHAHEL – Mission
1:40 – 2:00 | 42 MIKAEL – Political Authority & Order
2:00 – 2:20 | 43 VEULIAH – Prosperity
2:20 – 2:40 | 44 YELAHIAH – Karmic Warrior
2:40 – 3:00 | 45 SEALIAH – Motivation & Willfulness
3:00 – 3:20 | 46 ARIEL – Perceiver & Revealer
3:20 – 3:40 | 47 ASALIAH – Contemplation
3:40 – 4:00 | 48 MIHAEL – Fertility & Fruitfulness
4:00 – 4:20 | 49 VEHUEL – Elevation & Grandeur
4:20 – 4:40 | 50 DANIEL – Eloquence
4:40 – 5:00 | 51 HAHASIAH – Universal Medicine
5:00 – 5:20 | 52 IMAMIAH – Expiation of Errors
5:20 – 5:40 | 53 NANAEL – Spiritual Communication
5:40 – 6:00 | 54 NITHAEL – Rejuvenation & Eternal Youth
6:00 – 6:20 | 55 MEBAHIAH – Intellectual Lucidity
6:20 – 6:40 | 56 POYEL – Fortune & Support
6:40 – 7:00 | 57 NEMAMIAH – Discernment
7:00 – 7:20 | 58 YEIALEL – Mental Force
7:20 – 7:40 | 59 HARAHEL – Intellectual Richness
7:40 – 8:00 | 60 MITZRAEL – Internal Reparation
8:00 – 8:20 | 61 UMABEL – Affinity & Friendship
8:20 – 8:40 | 62 IAH– HEL – Desire to Know
8:40 – 9:00 | 63 ANAUEL – Perception of Unity
9:00 – 9:20 | 64 MEHIEL – Vivification (Invigorate/Enliven)
9:20 – 9:40 | 65 DAMABIAH – Fountain of Wisdom
9:40 – 10:00 | 66 MANAKEL – Knowledge of Good & Evil
10:00 – 10:20 | 67 EYAEL – Transformation to Sublime
10:20 – 10:40 | 68 HABUHIAH – Healing
10:40 – 11:00 | 69 ROCHEL – Restitution
11:00 – 11:20 | 70 JABAMIAH – Alchemy (Transformation)
11:20 – 11:40 | 71 HAIYAEL – Divine Warrior & Weaponry
11:40 – 12:00 | 72 MUMIAH – Endings & Rebirth

Appendix II

Certain Aspects of the Kabbalah and the 72 Angels Tradition

The 72 Angels and Tree of Life tradition introduced in my first *Birth Angels* book in 2004 has strong connections to the 12th century work of Rabbi Yitzhak Ha-Ivver (Isaac the Blind) in Provence, France (c. 1160–1235), which was reportedly carried forward and further developed by Rabbi Moses ben Nahman (Nachmanides, or RaMBaN) (1194-1270) and other Rabbis and scholars into 13th-15th century Gerona, Spain. Although these men were working within the **Judaic Kabbalah**, there were notable influences and contributions from other mystical traditions, which give philosophical input to the Angelic aspects of the tradition: **Christian Gnosticism** (direct knowing of God through personal communion), **Sufism** (coming closer to the "inner Beloved" while still in life through love and unity-identification), **Hinduism** (the many "gods" as the many aspects of the "One Supreme Being" dwelling within and awaiting our recognition), **Neoplatonism** (espousing the "One" and the "Infinite" beyond being, from which all Life is brought forth containing the essence of the Divine One) and **Hermetics** (the Egyptian and Greek spiritual alchemy of transforming base *mettle* into the gold of wisdom and ennobled beingness in order to manifest Heaven on Earth). The spiritual pioneers of the Middle Ages and Renaissance who hailed from different paths believed in the right of all humankind – both men and women of all creeds and cultures – to have direct communion with the Divine without the dictates, prohibitions or exclusivities of dogma. This became an increasingly heretical notion as Europe approached the wide and terrible reach of the Spanish Inquisition that began in 1478.

The Spanish connection from medieval to modern times. In the 13th century, Nachmanides founded a yeshiva for Judaic and Kabbalah studies in Gerona (also "Girona"), Spain. He was a disciple of Kabbalist Rabbi Azriel of Girona, who himself was a disciple of Rabbi Isaac the Blind. Nachmanides was renowned for chronicling much of the oral tradition of the Kabbalah, as well as defending the Jewish position on Messianic doctrine in the court of King James I of Aragon in the famous Barcelona Dispute of 1263. He was subsequently forced into exile and passed the rest of his life in Israel. In 1492 the school and Jewish grotto were walled up and abandoned during the Conversion/Expulsion Edict of the Spanish Inquisition in which Jews were forced to convert to Christianity or flee. Many of those working with the Kabbalah fled to Safed, Israel, which yielded the works and influence in the 16th century of Rabbis Moshe Cordovero and Isaac Luria (the "ARI"), considered to be the fathers of modern Kabbalist thought. Today there is still a thriving arts and Kabbalah community in Safed.

In the meantime, the Gerona grotto (the "Call" or "Cahal") remained hidden for almost five centuries until a gentrification trend in the 1970's and 80's spurred interest in acquiring and renovating medieval properties. According to accounts given by Gerona historian, Assumpcio Hosta, to Dartmouth professors and travel writers, Myrna Katz Frommer and Harvey Frommer, restauranteur Joseph Tarres in the 1980's had acquired a number of properties in the grotto for the purpose of building a restaurant. During the excavations he found the remains of a medieval school which he subsequently learned had been the 13th century yeshiva founded by Nachmanides.

As recounted by Ms. Hostas, who ultimately became director of the Bonastruc ca Porta excavation project (to honor the Catalan name of Nachmanides), curiosity by the locals eventually turned into commitment as continued excavations revealed that there was once a thriving medieval Kabbalah community in Gerona that gave it a unique standing as the center of mystical Judaism in Spain. Medieval manuscripts which had remain untouched for centuries led to the discovery of hidden Hebrew parchments, and cooperations began with Yeshiva University in New York and the Museum of the Diaspora in Tel Aviv for research, cataloging and translation, which remain ongoing. www.travel-watch.com/spanish-jewish-con.htm and www.dartmouth.edu/~frommer/s_j_connection.htm

In the meantime, Kabaleb (Enrique Llop, 1927-1991), a Gerona native who was a journalist, author, Master Freemason, esoteric astrologer and founder of E.T.U, Escuela Transcendentalista Universal (School of Universal Transcendence), had already been deeply involved in working with the Kabbalah, referencing the lineage of Isaac the Blind, Nachmanides, Lazar Lenain (1793-1877) and others. Kabaleb also worked with renowned 20th century philosopher, teacher and esoteric astrologer, Omraam Mikhaël Aïvanhov (1900-1986), who lectured extensively on the mysteries of bringing the Kingdom of God to Earth within the individual through the mysteries of the Christ and aspects of Esoteric Christianity. Aïvanhov's recorded lectures by the Prosveta Society also include illuminations on the Tree of Life and the Divine mysteries, the Angels, astrology, alchemy, unity and more.

In addition to Aïvanhov's influence, Kabaleb especially referenced Lenain on the 72 Angels and their astrological correspondences, and developed it further into a more detailed Kabbalistic astrology which he outlined in his book *Les Anges* (Editions Bussiere 1989). As a boyhood friend and spiritual teacher of François Bernad-Termes (Haziel), some of Kabaleb's works on the 72 Angels were published in France under Haziel's name when Haziel moved to France from Gerona. Since Kabaleb's death in 1991, three of his four children carry on his legacy through their own work in the Kabbalah, astrology and esoteric healing modalities, as well as the publishing of Kabaleb's additional works: Soleika Llop, www.alchemiagenetica.com.es, Milena Llop, www.redmilenaria.com, and Tristan Llop, www.nuevavibracion.com). Thanks to my connection with Kabaleb's children through Linda Wheeler Bryant in Madrid, Spain, I am able to more accurately understand the contributions of Kabaleb in helping to revive and illuminate certain aspects of the 72 Angels tradition.

My own years of research of the Kabbalah tradition include certain works by Kabaleb and his influences, as well as multi-traditional sources spanning over 2500 years. I was initially introduced to the 72 Angels aspect of the tradition around 1996-97 by French Canadian and Swiss-French teachers Kaya and Christiane Muller, who now work with the 72 Angels and dream symbology (www.ucm.ca/en/info/the-72-angels). As my interest in the tradition grew because of its similarities to Christian mysticism, I continued with my own explorations, ultimately leading to the publication of *Birth Angels ~ Fulfilling Your Life Purpose with the 72 Angels of the Kabbalah* (2004 Andrews McMeel/Simon & Schuster).

A few years later I was contacted by Chairman Mike Booth of Aura-Soma® in the U.K. and learned that he and ASIACT (Art and Science International Academy of Colour Technologies) had developed their courses on the 72 Angels of the Kabbalah based on some of the material in my book. Finding similarities between the 72 Angels tradition and the philosophies developed by Aura-Soma founder Vicky Wall and her successor Mike Booth (including influences from Rudolph Steiner, Goethe, Isaac Newton and others), Aura-Soma associated their consciousness-philosophies and colour-therapy products and with the 72 Angels wisdoms. During my subsequent 2+ years of working with Aura-Soma, I did extensive research, together with Dr. Sundar Robert Dreyfus, on the transliterated spellings of the Angels' names, which vary through the ages because of Jewish migrations and permutations of dialect from one culture to another. As a result, Aura-Soma now uses different spellings on some of the Angels' names than I use in my own work, which are derived mostly from the texts of Kabaleb and Lenain.

Important Kabbalah texts and influences. People are often surprised to learn that there is no one definitive Kabbalah holy book or text. The Kabbalah, which means "the receiving," was for centuries a mystical oral tradition that was developed within, but somewhat hidden from, Judaic doctrine and everyday practice. It is largely based on esoteric and oral revelations, studies of ancient wisdoms, inspired texts and inner receivings passed down through the ages from Rabbis, mystics and scholars to the next generation of disciples and students. The earliest known Kabbalah work, from either the 2nd century BCE or CE and arguably attributed to Abraham or Moses, is the ***Sefer Yetzirah*** ("Book of Creation"). This is a short but intense mystical treatise about how the utterances of the first "Creator Sounds," which ultimately became known as the Hebrew Alphabet, brought about Creation. It is the cosmology in this ancient work that Kabbalists through the ages have referred to in their understanding of the nature of the Divine and the act of Creation.

Another prominent work is the ***Sefer Ha-Bahir*** (Book of Illumination), first published in Provence, France in 1176 and arguably attributed to oral illuminations by Isaac the Blind. This is a collection of parables about a quote attributed to Rabbi Nehunya ben Ha-Kana, a Talmudic sage of the 1st century. A third work, the ***Zohar*** (Book of Splendor), is arguably attributed to Moses de Leon in the 13th century as possibly a compilation of the teachings of Rabbi Shimon bar Yochai from the 2nd century. This work has had strong influence on Judaic thought and doctrine.

During the Renaissance, a Christian Cabala emerged as some Christian scholars saw similarities between the mystical aspects of Christian theology and Jewish mysticism, but this has never gained traction in mainstream Christianity. A more popular Hermetic Qabalah was developed, however, which incorporated aspects from most of the esoteric influences of the time, including the hidden magical side of the Jewish Kabbalah, Western astrology, alchemy (from Greco-Egyptian influences), pagan (earth) religions, Neoplatonism, Gnosticism, Rosicrucianism, Freemasonry and more. Judaic and Hermetic Kabbalah/Qabalah became widely commingled in Renaissance thought, quintessentially in the work of Henry Cornelius Agrippa (1486-1535) with his *Three Books of Occult Philosophy*. In the 19th century, the Hermetic Order of the Golden Dawn developed the Hermetic Qabalah further within Masonic and Rosicrucian structures. Other influences were Francis Barrett's *The Magus* (1801), Eliphas Levi (1810-1875), Aleister Crowley with his "New Aeon" approach (*Liber 777*), Dion Fortune (*The Mystical Kabbalah*) and many more as the 19th century moved into the 20th.

In the latter "new age" of the 20th century, as the Kabbalah became popular among modern and new age seekers looking for alternate spiritual paths, many new Kabbalah works began to emerge illuminating various aspects of both the Judaic and Hermetic traditions. Some of these are scholarly works, presenting traditional views of the Tree of Life, the mystical meanings of the Hebrew Alphabet and more – and many others explore the tradition through symbolism, psychology, biology, hermetics, "magick" and other aspects. One of my favorite works is *Simple Kabbalah*, by Kim Zetter, for its clear, lay-friendly and relatively short presentation of the important elements, aspects and history of the Judaic Kabbalah, including formative texts and certain Rabbis and Kabbalists who illuminated and preserved the tradition throughout time. However, except for certain works of the Kabbalah Centre and the Bergs, who hint at it from a different angle, "*The 72 Names of God*," the 72 Angels tradition has remained largely unknown.

The 72 Angels Tradition

The 72 Angels are understood by Kabbalists working with the Tree of Life symbology as energetic expressions, or embodied light-forms of the 72 Names, Being and Qualities of the Divine Itself. While some thinking regards the hierarchies of Angels as created beings, the Angelic Tree of Life mysteries say that the 72 Angels are the initial *emanations* of the Divine Itself, revealing and energetically embodying the inherent diversity of Its nature. This is possibly a correspondence to what certain ancient Judeo-Christian literatures call "Angels of the Presence" which came forth on the "first day" and were said to represent the faces of God, as God Itself.

This tradition is compelling because there is a kind of spiritual science and ageless but exacting wisdom to it that calls us to an Angel-assisted practice of inner engagement with the Divine through feeling, direct knowing and interaction. While the tradition does not espouse or exclude religion, it has the capacity to re-enliven any religion or path since it contains aspects that are found in the mystical hearts of most, if not all, traditions. The foundational premise of the 72 Angels and Tree of Life tradition is that God is within us and we are within God, and both the Divine and the Human are evolving and expanding together through Divine-Human beingness and co-creation on Earth. Our work with the 72 Angels addresses the deepest longings we hold in our hearts for identity, meaning and purpose. Thus, it is the heart where these "angles" of Divine Light do their most transformational work within us – and so, in collaboration with the Angelically Divine, the human heart is the portal that brings "Heaven to Earth."

The 12th-15th century Kabbalists worked with the Tree of Life as a universal flow chart for the differentiation and "descent" of the Divine Oneness into the hierarchies of the 72 Angels and ultimately all of Creation. As a template for universal man, the Tree presents the 72 Angels as key "connectors" in the mysteries of the Divine-Human two-way relationship that happens within us. As the 72 Angels amplify the Divine within the soul-heart-mind-body of human beingness, we return to our Divine roots inwardly through transformation and symbolic ascendance back up the Angelic Tree into higher consciousness.

The Tree of Life symbology was developed from the mystical "codes" in the *Sefer Yetzirah* and other early revelatory sources. Later, from a decoding of the Bible's *Exodus*, chapter 14, verses 19-21, the 72 Angels' names were discerned. As medieval and Renaissance Kabbalists began relating the astrological and spiritual sciences to the Angels and their roles in human life, associations were made to the Zodiacal degrees, planets and signs, and ultimately dates and times.

Considered to be as "birth-gifts" of the Divine Light-essence acting from within and among us, the 72 Angels illuminate and amplify the vast spectrum of Divine possibilities and purposes within humanity. Furthermore, our personal Birth Angels (which correspond to our date and time of birth) especially signify and support what we each are here to do, heal, express and manifest in our current lifetime. Possibly the most comprehensive illumination of the deeper nature of the Angels and their roles in our lives, the 72 Angels tradition makes these distinctions that go far beyond the understandings about angels in modern angelogy:

As "angles" of Divine Light which amplify Divine consciousness within our humanity, it is said that the 72 Angels are not created beings, but emanations of the Divine Itself into 72 "angles" of Divine Light refracted into hues, or qualities, of the Divine. Thus, as aspects of Divine Light dwelling within us, the Angels amplify in each of us the particular light-qualities of the Divine which they embody and which our soul has chosen to manifest in our current lifetime through our physical, emotional and mental qualities, potentials and purposes.

As amplifiers of the awareness that we are not "only human, but Divine-Human beings, the Angels show us that God is everywhere, in the inside and outside of everything and every one. Thus, God, and all that is Divine, is not separate and apart from us, but rather here, among and within each of us as a differentiated soul-spark of Itself that animates and gives meaning and purpose to our human form, being and doing. So we are composed of both inner and outer realities that makes us both Divine *and* human.

As illuminators of the Love and Truth which compose our Divine soul nature, the Angels show us that our souls, as sparks of the Divine Itself, are composed of the Truth of the Divine "I AM" and the creation energy of Love which expands and manifests Truth into visible and relatable forms. Thus, the Angels awaken and amplify the particular aspects of love and truth which we each carry in our souls, so that the truth of who we are might be continually increased and manifested through the energies and resources of love. This is why there is so much energy around our earthly purposes, endeavors and creations that are propelled by love.

As "heart-bridge" builders within us and two-way messengers between our Divine and human aspects, the Angels work with and within our hearts to bring the love and truth held within our soul into our outer will and actions. The Angels show us that the heart is the broadcaster of the soul and the "inner cauldron" in which our Divine and Human aspects are commingled. Here at the sacred altar of our hearts is where the 72 Angelic aspects of the Divine meet the particular needs, longings, hurts, challenges, potentials and purposes of our humanity. Simply put, the Angels help the soul to talk to the heart, and the heart to talk to mind and body. As the Angels amplify our soul-light, its Divine qualities and purposes "spill over" into our heart as love, compassion, intuition, personal truth and wisdom – and then the Angels help to "turn up the volume" in the heart so that mind and body can hear. Looking at ourselves in this light, we can perhaps realize that the "little voice" of truth and intuition in our hearts is the Divine Itself, as our own soul, guiding us not from afar, but right here and now, from within.

In our two-way communication with the Divine, it is important to note that when we pray, we are doing two marvelous things – (1) quickening our awareness that we have the Divine "on tap" within our own souls to help with our human conditions and circumstances, and (2) tapping into the greater Divine consciousness in all of Creation and the cosmos in both time and the eternal. Thus, by plugging into our own inner Divine, we gain access to the totality of the Divine and the spiritual magic that can happen "when two or more are gathered!" This is why prayer-chains and group meditations and healings are so powerful.

As transformers of our base mettle into a goldenness of being, the "Angel alchemy" that takes place in our hearts helps to heal the "karma," or residue, of harbored hurts and issues so that we may be free to express the true "dharma" of our soul purposes in service to ourselves, each other and the Divine. You might say that the Angels are agents of the Divine Grace that only happens in our hearts, enabling us to make quantum leaps across eons of accumulated cause and effect to experience remarkable healing and transformation that can re-birth us into a new life. In this, they are as conveyors of the Christic energies of unconditional love and compassion.

As expressions of the diverse nature of the Divine, the Angels illuminate for us that it takes the totality of humankind and all the varieties of beings and things of the natural world and beyond to reveal and express the diverse nature of God. We are each and all manifestations of the greatest paradox in the universe: the endless diversity hidden within the greater reality of Oneness, revealed through Creation so that the Oneness might become knowable to Itself through relationship with Other. Having been created "in the image and likeness of God," isn't that same urge also within us as the desire to know and experience more of who we are through our relationships with others, including through all we ourselves create?

This suggests the importance of not just tolerating our own and each other's differences, but embracing ourselves and all beings, ways and things as valuable and illuminating pieces of the bigger picture puzzle of the Divine and Life Itself. Truly, we are each here to literally "flesh out" our part of the picture with the fullness of our true and unique being for the benefit of our own souls, each other and the fulfillment of the Divine on Earth.

BIRTH ANGELS BOOK OF DAYS

Daily Wisdoms with the 72 Angels of the Tree of Life

Volume 1: March 21 – June 2
Relationship with the Divine

Volume 2: June 3 – August 16
Relationship with Self

Volume 3: August 17 – October 29
Relationship with Work and Purpose

Volume 4: October 30 – January 8
Relationship with Others

Volume 5: January 9 – March 20
Relationship with Community and the World

Additional Offerings

Birth Angels ~ Fulfilling Your Life Purpose with the 72 Angels of the Kabbalah

Quick-Reference Charts & Posters:
The Kabbalah Tree of Life
72 Angels of the Tree of Life ~ Days & Hours of Support

"Daily Wisdoms" E-Mail Subscription

72 Angels Day-Keeper Journals

Speaking, Personal Coaching, Workshops

and more...

---

www.72BirthAngels.com | www.TerahCox.com

You are invited to share your experiences in working with the 72 Angels by contacting the author at
TerahCox@gmail.com

About the Author

TERAH COX has worked with the Kabbalah, Christianity, Sufism and aspects of other spiritual paths and wisdoms throughout her life in search of the common threads of Love and Truth in their mystical hearts. In addition to the five-volume series of *Birth Angels Book of Days*, she is the author of *The Story of Love & Truth*, *Birth Angels ~ Fulfilling Your Life Purpose with the 72 Angels of the Kabbalah*, *You Can Write Song Lyrics*, and more. She is also a speaker, coach and mentor on the subjects of individuation and life purposing, creativity, spiritual development and the balance of individuation and unity. Drawing from the fruits of "extraordinary listening," she has used her writings, teaching and coaching as ways of discovering and sharing the Divine-Human mysteries at play within every being, circumstance and aspect of life.

Formerly a writer for the Aura-Soma Colour-Care-System® in the U.K., she was also signed to the music publishing companies of Columbia Pictures, BMG Music, Warner-Chappell and various European music publishers as a lyric writer of over 150 songs recorded for CDs, film and television. Her inspirational poetry-art designs for wall-art, greeting cards, prints and more are online and in galleries and retail shops across the U.S.

* * *

Books & materials, speaking, coaching and workshops
www.72BirthAngels.com | www.TerahCox.com

Poetry art, greeting cards, prints & more
www.HeavenandEarthWorks.com

E-Cards with original music, messages and art
www.MilestonesConnect.com

Printed in Great Britain
by Amazon.co.uk, Ltd.,
Marston Gate.